SENSATIONAL
SALADS

SENSATIONAL
SALADS

DELICIOUS RECIPES FROM
AROUND THE WORLD

Consultant Editor: **Christine Ingram**

Sebastian Kelly

This edition published in 1999 by Sebastian Kelly

Produced by Anness Publishing Limited
Hermes House, 88-89 Blackfriars Road
London SE1 8HA

ISBN 1 84081 258 3

Publisher: Joanna Lorenz
Senior Cookery Editor: Linda Fraser
Project Editor: Anne Hildyard
Designer: Siân Keogh

Front cover: Lisa Tai, Designer; Thomas Odulate, Photographer;
Helen Trent, Stylist; Lucy McKelvie, Home Economist

Photography: Karl Adamson, David Armstong, Edward Allwright,
Steve Baxter, James Duncan, Amanda Heywood and Patrick McLeavey

Food for Photography: Jacqueline Clark, Kit Chan, Jane Hartshorn,
Jane Stevenson, Steven Wheeler and Carole Handslip

Stylists: Blake Minton and Kirsty Rawlings

Additional Recipes: Carla Capalbo and Laura Washburn

Previously published as *Classic Salads*

Printed in Hong Kong/China

1 3 5 7 9 10 8 6 4 2

NOTES
Standard spoon and cup measurements are level.

Medium eggs should be used unless otherwise stated.

CONTENTS

INTRODUCTION

Salads must be one of the most satisfying dishes to prepare. Visually, as well as in texture and flavor, they are ideal – colorful, fresh and varied. There's no limit to the fabulous salads an imaginative cook can create.

It is almost impossible to say what defines a salad. They are frequently made with raw ingredients, but cooked grains or other vegetables are equally in order. They are often served cold, but many are warm – perhaps served with a hot dressing or with grilled meat or fish. Their role in a meal is no clue either: salads make a perfect accompaniment, but almost every cuisine in the world has its favorite main course salad too – from Gado-Gado in Indonesia to Italy's excellent pasta salads. Perhaps a salad's most defining feature is the dressing. Classically this is made using oil and vinegar although all sorts of other ingredients can be used. However, the purpose is always the same – to unite all the separate elements of the salad into a glorious whole.

There are no rules on what can or cannot go into a salad, although green salad leaves are among the favorites. Vegetables and fruit, whether raw or cooked, should be absolutely fresh, while cooked ingredients like rice or pasta should be cooked *al dente*, so that they retain some bite to give the salad texture.

SALAD GREENS
Romaine lettuce – has a firm texture and slightly nutty flavor.
Bibb – has a firm heart and a distinct, pleasant flavor.
Frisée endive and *escarole* – are members of the chicory family. They have a distinct, slightly bitter flavor that is best combined with sweeter leaves like lamb's lettuce or iceberg.
Radicchio – is a member of the chicory family and has a similar bitter flavor. It is a favorite salad leaf, not only for its flavor but for its beautiful foliage – deep wine-red leaves and creamy ribs.
Belgian endive – is similar to escarole but has a slightly sweeter taste. It can withstand a strong dressing.
Iceberg lettuce – although fairly mild in flavor, this lettuce has a wonderful crunchy texture and is good mixed with more strongly flavored leaves, like frisée or watercress.
Lollo rosso – is a loose-leafed lettuce with a mild flavor. Valued for its superb purple-red foliage, this lettuce is best mixed with stronger flavored salad leaves.
Lollo biondo – is similar in flavor to lollo rosso, and has a pretty curly edge.

Oakleaf lettuce – is a loose-leafed lettuce with a mild pleasant flavor. The leaves range from pale green, through pink to a deep maroon.
Mâche (corn salad) – is a delicious, slightly sweet leaf that makes a wonderful addition to a salad, or can be used as a garnish by itself.
Arugula – is a deservedly popular leaf with a distinct lemon-pepper flavor. Add to milder flavored leaves, like iceberg or oakleaf lettuce.
Spinach – the young leaves make a wonderful salad, either mixed with other leaves or by themselves. They have an excellent rich flavor and are extremely nutritious, being a good source of vitamins A, B and C and iron, when eaten raw. Remove stalks if rough.
Watercress – is strong tasting with a peppery flavor. Excellent when combined with milder leaves.

OTHER SALAD VEGETABLES
While salad leaves often form the basis of a salad, almost all vegetables can be used, either as part of the salad, or in their own right. Many recipes have vegetables simply prepared and served raw, but sometimes they can be steamed or grilled to add an interesting and delicious dimension to a dish.
Celery – use white or green celery; remove the strings and slice finely.
Fennel – use raw; cut into fine julienne strips or blanch first and add to mixed salads. It has a distinct and sharp aniseed flavor and tastes best with blander vegetables, and with a creamy dressing.
Cucumber – with its clean, crisp texture, cucumber is excellent in many salad dishes with a strong dressing.

Clockwise from top left: Belgian endive, lollo rosso, lollo biondo, escarole, oakleaf lettuce, mâche, spinach, watercress, arugula, frisée, romaine, iceberg and Bibb.

Cabbage – very finely sliced white cabbage mixed with grated carrot makes the ever popular coleslaw.
Chinese cabbage – either served raw or briefly steamed or stir-fried, is popular in many Chinese or Thai salad dishes.
Carrots – with their wonderful sweet flavor, carrots are invaluable in salads. They can be grated and mixed with a caraway seed dressing, or cut into julienne strips for a variety of salads.
Zucchini – unless very young, when they only need to be thinly sliced, zucchini are best when briefly steamed with herbs. They too can have a starring role in a salad, dressed with a yogurt or sour cream dressing.
Onions and *green onions* – mild flavored onions, like red or Spanish onions, cut into thin rings are excellent in tomato salads, dressed with a good olive oil. Green onions are great in large salads, or added to a green salad.
Green beans – trim and then cook these for a few minutes, either steaming or boiling in a little bit of water until just tender. Drain and refresh under cold running water. Green beans make a superb salad by themselves, served with chopped tomatoes, onions and garlic, or they can be added to other green salads.
Asparagus – steam until tender and add to green salads for a luxurious flavor.
Mushrooms – provide texture to a salad. Fresh button mushrooms can be sliced and used in mixed salads or featured more prominently with peanuts or cashews and avocado or banana for an unusual but delicious side salad. Wipe clean with damp paper towels.
Tomatoes – an essential salad ingredient, added to mixed salads or better still given a starring role in salads like Salata Tricolore – tomatoes, mozzarella and fresh basil. Buy top quality tomatoes for salads, preferably those on the vine, which have the best flavor.
Avocado – with their soft texture and mild flavor, avocados make a wonderful addition to mixed green salads. Sprinkle the flesh with lemon juice after slicing to prevent it from discoloring.

A selection of vegetables for using in salads includes potatoes, celery, fennel, tomatoes, turnips, garlic, green onions, mushrooms, zucchini, baby corn, carrots and green beans.

Red and green bell peppers – these are another versatile salad vegetable. Slice them and add raw to bean salads or roast or grill them and serve with garlic, tomatoes and olive oil for a rich Italian salad. To roast peppers, char them under the broiler until the skin blackens and then place in a plastic bag. Close tightly and then when cool enough to handle, peel off the outer skin.

FRUIT

Fruit, of course, comes into its own in fruit salads, but there is a place for fruit in many savory salads as well – tomatoes, avocados and peppers are fruit, don't forget. When using fruit in salads, use it to complement other flavors. Apples, with their crisp texture and pleasant sweet taste are nice when combined with softer ingredients, such as avocado. Pears are excellent in all sorts of salads – try them with arugula or other strongly flavored leaves. Citrus fruits, such as oranges and grapefruit, add astringency to a salad. They also go well in pasta salads with fennel or celery, tossed with a creamy dressing that brings the flavors together. Fruit is particularly useful in elegant, large salads where each separate ingredient is prepared and laid out by itself. As well as adding color, their sweeter flavor contrasts with the more bitter salad ingredients. Mango and paw paw for instance, are essential in Gado-Gado, but also consider melons and grapes for antipasto.

USING HERBS

Herbs are as essential in salads as vegetables. Not only do they add their distinctive flavor, but when added to dressings or mayonnaise, they subtly change the character of a salad, so that you can enhance a particular flavor or stress a certain ingredient, simply by adding basil, or mint, for instance.

Many herbs can be added in whole sprigs to mixed green salads. Here they contrast with the flavor of other leaves, providing a delicious variety of tastes. Alternatively, herbs can be finely chopped and added to dressings, where they add a more diffuse flavor to the whole salad. Mint, for instance, sharpens a salad and is good with Turkish and Middle Eastern salads.

Herbs are invariably better when fresh, and nowadays it is easy to buy fresh herbs all year round. If you can grow your own, so much the better, and growing them in little window pots means you have a fresh supply for several weeks at a time.

Basil – with its pungent warm flavor, this is a favorite in many salads and essential for any Italian insalata. The leaves can be used whole and mixed into leafy salads, sprinkled over tomato salads and sprinkled with olive oil, or chopped and used in dressings.

Mint – unmistakable and clean tasting, mint adds freshness without masking other flavors. Use it in dressings, or finely chop it and add to salads.

Thyme – another of the warm, earthy herbs, with a characteristic blunt lemon flavor. Part of its appeal is its heady aroma which can be detected if used in dressings. Use thyme by itself or with parsley, garlic and marjoram.

Parsley – there are two main types of parsley: curly and flat leaf. Both have a fresh, faintly lemon flavor, more apparent in flat leaf parsley. Finely chopped, and used with marjoram, it adds a pleasant herby taste to dressings. Used in sprigs in salads, its characteristic flavor is more noticeable, and can enhance a plain green salad.

Clockwise from top left: thyme, flat leaf parsley, chives, lavender, rose petals, mint and basil.

Chives – unlike onions, to whose family they belong, chives have the virtue of having a flavor that doesn't take over the whole dish. Chives exemplify what's best about herbs – they add subtle reminders of other tastes, without cloaking other flavors. Chives can be snipped over salads or added to dressings and mayonnaise.

Marjoram – sweet and fragrant, the fresh leaves can be sprinkled onto salads, or added to dressings.

Tarragon – with its faintly aniseed and vanilla flavor, tarragon is best used in salads with fish or eggs, or used to flavor mayonnaise.

Cilantro – this fragrant herb is delicious added to mixed green salad adding a distinct pungency against the bitter frisée or sweet mâche. Store-bought cilantro from Indian markets can be very pungent indeed, but home-grown or locally grown cilantro is much milder. It's not so good in spicy dishes, but still wonderful in salads.

GARLIC

Garlic is mainly used as a flavoring – perhaps the most important one of all dressing ingredients. If very finely chopped, it can be sprinkled over tomato salads. However, garlic is mostly used in dressings, such as vinaigrette, mayonnaise, yogurt and herb. Don't use garlic indiscriminately, as it will take over given half the chance. However, for Provençal, Mediterranean or Greek salads, garlic is essential. To use in a dressing, crush a small bulb with the back of a knife, or use a garlic press if desired.

SPICES

While herbs add a subtle, fresh flavor to food, spices are more assertive, adding either pungency or heat and if used in moderation, bringing out the flavors of other ingredients. Spices should be used carefully, especially in salads, where flavors are delicate and can be overwhelmed by headier tastes.

Used carefully, however, you'll be surprised how a dash of ground coriander or a hint of cayenne pepper can enhance a salad or perk up a dressing, and for many Thai or Asian salads, a pinch of spice is essential.

Pepper

Pepper, either black or white, is the most popular spice in the Western hemisphere. It enhances the flavor of food by exciting the taste buds. The majority of savory dishes use a little pepper. Black pepper is milder than white. Always grind your own pepper, as already-ground pepper has a bland taste.

Celery salt – is a combination of celery seed and salt, and is useful in salads as it brings out the flavor of vegetables.

Cayenne pepper – is made from the dried, ground seeds and pods of the cayenne chili pepper. It is slightly less fiery than chili powder and can be used to spice up certain dressings.

Soy sauce – is made from fermented soy beans; light soy sauce is milder and less salty than the dark soy sauce. It is useful for adding body to dressings to go with pork, beef or duck salads.

Coriander – coriander seeds have a sweet orangey flavor, and ground coriander can be used in dressings for a fuller, more pungent flavor.

Other spices can be used sparingly in salads: cumin, cinnamon, cardamom and turmeric are all useful. If possible, always buy spices in small quantities, so that they do not sit around in the cupboard for years – or even months.

DRESSINGS

A dressing can make or break a salad. Well-made dressings should be a perfect blend of individual ingredients that harmonize with the leaves and vegetables, grains and meat or fish in the salad. Once you have spent time buying, preparing and arranging your salad, take extra time to make a well-flavored and balanced dressing.

OILS

Most dressings are made using oils. The dressing binds the salad together and oil is the principal element, adding richness in flavor and texture. Strongly flavored oils add a wonderful fragrance to a dressing, but their flavor needs to be tempered with milder oils.

Olive oil – this is the king of all oils, with a rich fragrance and flavor. The best olive oil is extra-virgin olive oil, where hand-picked olives are cold-pressed to give an almost perfect flavor. The olives for virgin olive oil are picked mechanically and often warmed before pressing for higher extraction of oil. Other standard olive oils are suitable for frying but for salads buy virgin or better still extra-virgin olive oil. For some dressings and for some palates, sunflower or safflower oil can be blended with olive oil for a milder but still satisfying flavor.

Seed oils – sunflower and safflower oil are mild, neutral oils, valued as such as they are useful as a base for stronger flavored oils. You can use half safflower, half olive oil for dressings, and mayonnaise can be made entirely with safflower oil, so that other flavors can be appreciated.

Nut oils – walnut and hazelnut oil have a distinct nutty flavor and make excellent dressings for certain salads. A little will go a long way and sunflower oil can be blended with nut oils with excellent results.

Garlic oil – make your own flavored oil by steeping 2–3 crushed garlic cloves in sunflower or if preferred, olive oil for 1–2 hours. This can then be used for frying croûtons or other ingredients where you would like a subtle garlic flavor.

OTHER DRESSING INGREDIENTS

Vinegars – unless a recipe calls for something particular, a simple white wine vinegar is all you need for most dressings and mayonnaise.

Lemon and lime juice – add astringency. Take care not to use too freely as they have a similar strength to vinegar.

Mustard – useful to add a depth of flavor and to act as an emulsifier. Dijon mustard, unless *fort*, is mild and suitable for most dressings, but English mustard is good when serving a salad with sausages or grilled meats.

MAKING SALADS

If making a mixed or leaf salad, choose leaves that give contrast in texture and color as well as flavor. Add fresh herbs for further contrasts in flavors.

MAKING DRESSINGS

Make a dressing in the proportion of five parts oil to one part vinegar or lemon juice. Season with salt and pepper and add French mustard and garlic according to the recipe or to preference. If desired, a pinch of sugar can also be added, which blunts the flavor. Dressings can be made using a whisk, in a blender or shaken in a jar.

From left: Italian olive oil, Spanish olive oil, Italian olive oil, safflower oil, hazelnut oil, walnut oil, peanut oil, French olive oil, Italian olive oil, wine vinegar and garlic oil.

APPETIZERS

*Salads are a perfect way to start a meal. Leafy salads combined
with a seafood cocktail, cheese or spicy meats are deliciously tasty,
but are still light enough to complement the main course. Smoked
Trout Salad or Egg and Tomato Salad with Crab are both favorite
starters: simple to prepare, yet fittingly attractive and elegant enough
for any dinner party. For a more substantial appetizer, or possibly
a light lunch, try Summer Tuna Salad or Spinach Salad
with Bacon and Shrimp.
Alternatively, mix and match various salads for
an intriguing buffet spread.*

Egg and Tomato Salad with Crab

Chili sauce and horseradish give this dressing a pleasant piquancy.

INGREDIENTS

Serves 4
lettuce leaves
2 cans (7 ounces each) crabmeat, drained
4 hard-cooked eggs, sliced
16 cherry tomatoes, halved
½ green bell pepper,
　seeded and thinly sliced
6 black olives, pitted and sliced

For the dressing
1 cup mayonnaise
2 teaspoons fresh lemon juice
3 tablespoons chili sauce
½ green bell pepper, seeded and finely
　chopped
1 teaspoon prepared horseradish
1 teaspoon Worcestershire sauce

1 To make the dressing, place all the ingredients in a bowl and mix well. Set aside in a cool place.

2 Line four plates with lettuce leaves. Mound the crabmeat in the center. Arrange the eggs around the outside with the tomatoes on top.

3 Spoon some of the dressing over the crabmeat. Arrange the green pepper slices on top and sprinkle with the olives. Serve immediately with the remaining dressing.

Summer Tuna Salad

This colorful salad is perfect for a summer lunch in the garden – use canned or freshly cooked salmon in place of the tuna, if desired.

INGREDIENTS

Serves 4–6
6 ounces radishes
1 cucumber
3 celery sticks
1 yellow bell pepper
6 ounces cherry tomatoes, halved
4 green onions, thinly sliced
3 tablespoons lemon juice
3 tablespoons olive oil
2 cans (7 ounces each) tuna, drained
　and flaked
2 tablespoons chopped fresh parsley
salt and freshly ground black pepper
lettuce leaves, to serve
thin strips twisted lemon rind, to
　garnish

1 Cut the radishes, cucumber, celery and yellow pepper into small cubes. Place in a large, shallow dish with the cherry tomatoes and green onions.

2 In a small mixing bowl, stir together the salt and lemon juice with a fork until dissolved. Pour this over the vegetable mixture. Add the oil and black pepper to taste. Stir to coat the vegetables. Cover and set aside for 1 hour.

3 Add the drained and flaked tuna and chopped parsley to the mixing bowl and toss gently until everything is well combined.

4 Arrange the lettuce leaves on a serving platter and spoon the salad into the center. Garnish with the strips of lemon rind.

Avocado and Papaya Salad

INGREDIENTS

Serves 4
2 ripe avocados
1 ripe papaya
1 large orange
1–2 ounces small arugula leaves
   or mâche
1 small red onion, thinly sliced

For the dressing
4 tablespoons olive oil
2 tablespoons lemon or lime juice
salt and freshly ground black pepper

1 Halve the avocados and remove the pits. Carefully peel off the skin, then cut each avocado half lengthwise into thick slices.

2 Peel and cut the papaya in half lengthwise. Scoop out the seeds and set aside 1 tablespoon for the dressing. Cut each papaya half into eight slices.

3 Peel the orange and cut out the segments, cutting on either side of the dividing membranes.

4 Combine the dressing ingredients in a small bowl and mix well. Stir in the reserved papaya seeds.

5 Assemble the salad on four individual serving plates. Alternate slices of papaya and avocado. Add the orange segments and a small mound of arugula topped with onion rings. Spoon on the dressing.

Mango, Tomato and Red Onion Salad

This salad makes a tempting appetizer; the mango has a subtle sweetness and the flavor blends well with the tomato.

INGREDIENTS

Serves 4
1 firm underripe mango
2 large tomatoes or 1 beefsteak tomato, sliced
½ red onion, sliced into rings
½ cucumber, peeled and thinly sliced
2 tablespoons sunflower or vegetable oil
1 tablespoon lemon juice
1 garlic clove, crushed
½ teaspoon hot pepper sauce
salt and freshly ground black pepper
sugar, to taste
snipped chives, to garnish

1 Cut away two thick slices on either side of the mango pit and cut into slices. Peel the skin from the slices.

2 Arrange the mango, tomato, onion and cucumber slices on a large serving plate.

3 Blend the oil, lemon juice, garlic, hot pepper sauce, salt and black pepper in a blender or food processor, or place in a small jar and shake vigorously. Add a pinch of sugar to taste and mix again.

4 Pour the dressing over the salad and garnish with snipped chives.

Spinach Salad with Bacon and Shrimp

Serve this hot salad with plenty of crusty bread for mopping up the delicious juices.

INGREDIENTS

Serves 4

7 tablespoons olive oil
½ tablespoon sherry vinegar
2 garlic cloves, finely chopped
1 teaspoon Dijon mustard
12 large shrimp, shelled and deveined
4 ounces lean bacon, cut into strips
about 4 ounces fresh young spinach
  leaves
½ head oakleaf lettuce, roughly torn
salt and freshly ground black pepper

1 To make the dressing, whisk together 6 tablespoons of the olive oil with the vinegar, garlic, mustard and seasoning in a small pan. Heat gently until thickened slightly, then keep warm.

2 Carefully peel the shrimp, leaving the tails intact. Set aside.

3 Heat the remaining oil in a frying pan and fry the bacon until browned and crisp, stirring occasionally. Add the shrimp and stir-fry for a few minutes until warmed through.

4 While the bacon and shrimp are cooking, arrange the spinach and torn oakleaf lettuce leaves on four individual serving plates.

5 Spoon the bacon and shrimp onto the leaves, then pour on the hot dressing. Serve immediately.

Smoked Trout Salad

Horseradish is as good a partner with smoked trout as it is with roast beef. In this recipe it combines with yogurt to make a delicious light salad dressing.

INGREDIENTS

Serves 4
1 oakleaf or other red lettuce
8 ounces small tomatoes, cut into thin wedges
½ cucumber, peeled and thinly sliced
4 smoked trout fillets (about 7 ounces each), skinned and flaked

For the dressing
pinch of English mustard powder
3–4 teaspoons white wine vinegar
2 tablespoons light olive oil
scant ¾ cup plain yogurt
2 tablespoons grated fresh or bottled horseradish
pinch of sugar

COOK'S TIP

Salt should not be necessary in this recipe because of the saltiness of the trout.

1 First, make the dressing: Combine the mustard powder and vinegar, then gradually whisk in the oil, yogurt, horseradish and sugar. Set aside for 30 minutes.

2 Place the lettuce leaves in a large bowl. Stir the dressing again, then pour half of it over the leaves and toss lightly using two spoons.

3 Arrange the lettuce on four individual plates with the tomatoes, cucumber and trout. Spoon on the remaining dressing and serve at once.

Mushroom Salad

This is a simple and refreshing salad. Letting it stand for a few hours before serving brings out the sweetness of the mushrooms.

INGREDIENTS

Serves 4

6 ounces button mushrooms
grated zest and juice of ½ lemon
2–3 tablespoons crème fraîche or sour cream
salt and white pepper
1 tablespoon snipped fresh chives, to garnish

COOK'S TIP

If you prefer, toss the mushrooms in a little vinaigrette – made by whisking 4 tablespoons walnut oil or extra virgin olive oil into the lemon juice.

1 Trim and slice the mushrooms thinly and place in a mixing bowl. Add the lemon zest and juice and the cream, adding a little more cream if needed. Stir gently to mix, then season with salt and white pepper. Let the salad stand for at least 1 hour.

2 Stir occasionally, then serve sprinkled with snipped chives.

Creamy Mâche and Beet Salad

This salad makes a colorful and unusual starter.

INGREDIENTS

Serves 4

5–6 ounces mâche, washed and roots trimmed
3 or 4 small beets, cooked, peeled and diced
2 tablespoons chopped fresh parsley

For the vinaigrette

2–3 tablespoons white wine vinegar or lemon juice
1 heaping tablespoon Dijon mustard
2 garlic cloves, finely chopped
½ tablespoon sugar
½ cup sunflower or safflower oil
½ cup crème fraîche or heavy or whipping cream
salt and freshly ground black pepper

1 First, make the vinaigrette. Mix the vinegar or lemon juice, mustard, garlic, sugar, salt and pepper in a small bowl, then slowly whisk in the oil until the sauce thickens.

2 Lightly beat the crème fraîche or heavy cream to lighten it slightly, then whisk it into the vinaigrette.

3 Toss the lettuce with a little of the vinaigrette and arrange on a serving plate or in a bowl.

4 Spoon the beets into the center of the lettuce and drizzle on the remaining vinaigrette. Sprinkle with parsley and serve immediately.

Raw Vegetables with Olive Oil Dip

This healthy starter from Rome uses only the very best olive oil and salt.

Ingredients

Serves 6–8
3 large carrots, peeled
2 fennel bulbs
6 celery stalks
1 red bell pepper, cored and seeded
2 large tomatoes or 12 cherry tomatoes
8 green onions
12 radishes, trimmed
12 small cauliflower florets

For the dip
½ cup extra virgin olive oil
3 tablespoons fresh lemon juice and 4 fresh basil leaves, torn into small pieces
salt and freshly ground black pepper

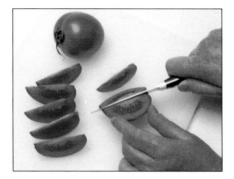

1 Prepare the vegetables by slicing the carrots, fennel, celery and pepper into small sticks.

2 If using large tomatoes, cut into sections, or leave cherry tomatoes whole. Trim the roots and dark green leaves from the onions. Arrange all the vegetables on a large platter, leaving space in the center for the dip.

3 Make the dip by pouring the olive oil into a small bowl. Add salt and pepper and stir in the lemon juice and basil. Place the bowl in the center of the vegetable platter.

Celery Stuffed with Gorgonzola

If possible, prepare this dish just before serving.

Ingredients

Serves 4–6
12 crisp celery stalks, leaves left on
½ cup Gorgonzola cheese
½ cup cream cheese
snipped fresh chives, to garnish

1 Wash and dry the celery stalks and trim the root ends.

2 In a small bowl, mash the cheeses together until smooth.

3 Fill the celery stalks with the cheese mixture, using a spatula to smooth the filling. Chill for 30–45 minutes before serving. Garnish with snipped chives.

> ——— Cook's Tip ———
>
> Use another soft and creamy blue cheese in place of the Gorgonzola, if you prefer – or choose a strong flavored Cheddar and grate it before adding to the cream cheese.

MAIN COURSE SALADS

Give a salad center stage in a meal and you're likely to find that it is not only star of the show, but one of the leading lights of your whole repertoire. Salads such as Seafood Salad with Fragrant Herbs or Tangy Chicken Salad are among the most perfectly balanced meals – meat, fish, cheese or lentils give the necessary protein, while the vegetables provide a wide range of essential vitamins and minerals. A satisfying salad should also contain beans, potatoes, rice or pasta, and even if you are planning a low-calorie meal, don't skimp on carbohydrates, but just leave out rich dressings. Use a low-fat dressing, or a dressing of finely chopped herbs, together with lemon and lime juice, which provides flavor without the calories.

Warm Salmon Salad

Guests will love this light refreshing salad. Serve it for lunch or on a summer's evening.

INGREDIENTS

Serves 4

1 salmon fillet (about 1 pound), skinned
2 tablespoons sesame oil
grated zest of ½ orange
juice of 1 orange
1 tablespoon Dijon mustard
1 tablespoon chopped fresh tarragon
3 tablespoons peanut oil
4 ounces fine green beans, trimmed
6 ounces mixed salad greens, such as young spinach, radicchio, frisée and romaine lettuce leaves
1 tablespoon sesame seeds
salt and freshly ground black pepper

1 Cut the salmon into bite-size pieces, then make the dressing. Combine the sesame oil, orange zest and juice, mustard, chopped tarragon and seasoning in a bowl. Set aside.

2 Heat the peanut oil in a frying pan. Add the salmon pieces and fry for 3–4 minutes, until lightly browned but still tender inside.

3 While the salmon is cooking, blanch the green beans in boiling salted water for 5–6 minutes, until tender yet crisp.

4 Add the dressing to the fried salmon, toss gently and cook for 30 seconds. Remove the pan from the heat.

5 Arrange the salad leaves on four serving plates. Drain the beans and toss them over the leaves. Spoon onto the salmon with the cooking juices and serve immediately, sprinkled with the sesame seeds.

Shrimp and Artichoke Salad

Artichokes and shrimp are a popular combination in the Southern states of America. This particular salad comes from Louisiana and the sharp, garlicky dressing is a typical Creole flavor.

INGREDIENTS

Serves 4
1 garlic clove
2 tablespoons Dijon mustard
4 tablespoons red wine vinegar
¾ cup olive oil
3 tablespoons shredded fresh basil leaves
2 tablespoons finely chopped
   fresh parsley
1 red onion, very finely sliced
12 ounces cooked shelled shrimp
1 can (14 ounces) artichoke hearts
½ head iceberg lettuce
salt and freshly ground black pepper

1 Chop the garlic, then crush it to a pulp with 1 tablespoon salt, using the flat side of a heavy knife.

2 Blend the garlic and mustard to a paste, then add the vinegar and finally the olive oil, beating well to make a thick creamy dressing. Season with black pepper and, if necessary, a little more salt.

3 Add the basil or parsley and then stir in the sliced onion. Let stand for 30 minutes at room temperature, stir in the shrimp and chill in the fridge for 1 hour or until ready to serve.

4 Drain the artichoke hearts and halve each one. Shred the iceberg lettuce finely.

5 Make a bed of lettuce on a serving platter or on four individual salad plates and arrange the artichoke hearts on top.

6 Just before serving, spoon the shrimp and onion over the artichoke salad and then pour the marinade over the top.

Seafood Salad with Fragrant Herbs

INGREDIENTS

Serves 4–6

1 cup fish stock or water
12 ounces squid, cleaned and cut into
  rings
12 uncooked jumbo shrimp, shelled
12 scallops
2 ounces bean thread noodles, soaked
  in warm water for 30 minutes
juice of 1–2 limes
2 tablespoons fish sauce
½ cucumber, cut into thin sticks
1 stalk lemongrass, finely chopped
2 kaffir lime leaves, finely shredded
2 shallots, finely sliced
2 tablespoons chopped green onion
2 tablespoons chopped fresh cilantro
12–15 mint leaves, roughly torn
3–4 red chilies, seeded and sliced
sprigs of fresh cilantro, to garnish

1 Pour the stock into a medium-size saucepan, set over a high heat and bring to a boil.

2 Cook each type of seafood separately in the stock. Don't overcook – it takes only a few minutes for each. Drain and set aside.

3 Drain the bean thread noodles and cut them into short lengths, about 2 inches long. Combine the noodles with the cooked seafood.

4 Blend the lime juice and fish sauce and mix with the cucumber, lemongrass, kaffir lime leaves, shallots, green onions, herbs and chilies. Toss with the seafood and noodles and spoon on to a large serving platter. Garnish with cilantro and serve.

COOK'S TIP

Kaffir lime leaves, also known as citrus or lime leaves, have a unique flavor. They are available fresh or dried at most Asian markets.

Pomelo Salad

A pomelo is a type of citrus fruit, with a sharp but sweet flesh.

INGREDIENTS

Serves 4–6
For the dressing
2 tablespoons Thai fish sauce
1 tablespoon sugar
2 tablespoons lime juice

For the salad
2 tablespoons vegetable oil
4 shallots, finely sliced
2 garlic cloves, finely sliced
1 large pomelo or pink grapefruit
1 tablespoon roasted peanuts
4 ounces cooked shelled shrimp
4 ounces fresh cooked crabmeat
10–12 small mint leaves
2 green onions, finely sliced
2 red chilies, seeded and finely sliced,
  fresh cilantro leaves and shredded
  fresh coconut (optional), to garnish

1 Whisk together the fish sauce, sugar and lime juice and set aside.

2 Heat the oil in a small frying pan, add the shallots and garlic and fry until lightly brown. Transfer with a slotted spoon to a plate.

3 Peel the grapefruit and break the flesh into small pieces, taking care to remove all the membranes.

4 Coarsely grind the peanuts into a large bowl, then add the grapefruit, shrimp, crabmeat, mint leaves and the fried shallot mixture. Add the dressing and toss well to mix. Arrange on a serving plate and sprinkle with the green onions, red chilies, cilantro leaves and shredded coconut, if using.

Shrimp and Tuna Salad

INGREDIENTS

Serves 4

4 ounces cooked peeled shrimp
1 garlic clove, crushed
½ tablespoon vegetable oil
2 hard-cooked eggs
1 plantain, halved
a few lettuce leaves
2 tomatoes
1 red bell pepper, seeded
1 avocado
juice of 1 lemon
1 carrot
1 can (7 ounces) tuna or sardines
1 green chili, seeded and finely
    chopped
2 tablespoons chopped green onion
salt and freshly ground black pepper

1 Put the shrimp in a bowl; add the garlic and a little seasoning.

2 Heat the oil in a small saucepan, add the shrimp and cook over low heat for a few minutes. Transfer to a plate to cool.

3 Shell and cut the hard-cooked eggs into slices.

4 Boil the plantain in a pan of water for 15 minutes, cool, then peel and slice thickly.

5 Shred the lettuce and arrange on a large serving plate. Slice the tomatoes and red pepper and peel and slice the avocado, sprinkling it with a little lemon juice. Cut the carrot into matchstick-size pieces and arrange over the lettuce with the other vegetables.

6 Add the plantain, eggs, shrimp and tuna fish. Sprinkle with the remaining lemon juice, scatter the chili and green onion on top and season with salt and pepper to taste. Serve as a lunch-time salad or as a delicious side dish.

COOK'S TIP

For a more substantial salad, use more shrimp. Any types of lettuce can be used. Choose a variety of leaves for interesting color and flavor.

Tangy Chicken Salad

Thai cuisine often features fresh salad greens, together with water chestnuts, herbs and nuts combined with spicy poultry or fish. The chicken is marinated and grilled before being sliced, and the coconut and lime dressing brings the two elements together in perfect harmony.

INGREDIENTS

Serves 4–6

4 skinned, boneless chicken breasts
2 garlic cloves, crushed
2 tablespoons soy sauce
2 tablespoons vegetable oil
½ cup coconut milk
2 tablespoons Asian fish sauce
juice of 1 lime
2 tablespoons sugar
4 ounces water chestnuts, sliced
2 ounces cashews, roasted
4 shallots, finely sliced
4 kaffir lime leaves, finely sliced
1 stalk lemongrass, finely sliced
1 tablespoon finely chopped galangal or
   fresh ginger
1 large red chili, seeded and finely sliced
2 green onions, finely sliced
10–12 mint leaves, torn
1 head lettuce, shredded
sprigs of cilantro, to garnish
2 red chilies, seeded and sliced, to garnish

1 Trim the chicken breasts of any excess fat and put them in a large dish. Rub with the garlic, soy sauce and 1 tablespoon of the oil. Marinate for 1–2 hours.

2 Grill the chicken for 4–5 minutes on both sides, until cooked.

3 In a small saucepan, heat the coconut milk, fish sauce, lime juice and sugar. Stir until all of the sugar has dissolved and then remove from the heat.

4 Cut the cooked chicken into strips and mix with the water chestnuts, cashews, shallots, kaffir lime leaves, lemongrass, galangal, red chili, green onions and mint leaves.

5 Pour the coconut dressing over the chicken mixture and stir well. Spread lettuce over a large serving plate and spoon the chicken mixture on top. Garnish with sprigs of cilantro and sliced red chilies.

——— COOK'S TIP ———

Galangal is a member of the ginger family and looks very similar to ginger. If it's not available at Asian stores, use fresh ginger instead.

Spicy Szechuan Noodle Salad

INGREDIENTS

Serves 4

12 ounces thick egg noodles
6 ounces cooked chicken, shredded
2 ounces roasted cashews

For the dressing

4 green onions, chopped
2 tablespoons chopped fresh cilantro
2 garlic cloves, minced
2 tablespoons smooth peanut butter
2 tablespoons sweet chili sauce
1 tablespoon soy sauce
1 tablespoon sherry vinegar
1 tablespoon sesame oil
2 tablespoons olive oil
2 tablespoons chicken stock or water
10 toasted Szechuan peppercorns, ground

1 Cook the noodles in a saucepan of boiling water until just tender, following the directions on the package. Drain, rinse under cold running water and drain well.

2 While the noodles are cooking, combine all the ingredients for the dressing in a large bowl and whisk together well.

3 Add the noodles, shredded chicken and cashews to the dressing, toss gently to coat and adjust the seasoning to taste. Serve immediately.

— COOK'S TIP —

You could substitute cooked turkey or pork for the chicken for a change.

Sesame Noodle Salad with Green Onions

This simple but very tasty warm salad can be prepared and cooked in just a few minutes.

INGREDIENTS

Serves 4

2 garlic cloves, coarsely chopped
2 tablespoons tahini
1 tablespoon dark sesame oil
2 tablespoons soy sauce
2 tablespoons rice wine
1 tablespoon clear honey
pinch of five-spice powder
12 ounces soba or buckwheat noodles
4 green onions, finely sliced diagonally
2 ounces bean sprouts
3-inch piece of cucumber, cut into matchsticks
toasted sesame seeds
salt and freshly ground black pepper

1 Process the garlic, tahini, oil, soy sauce, rice wine, honey and five-spice powder with a pinch each of salt and pepper in a blender or food processor until smooth.

2 Cook the noodles in a saucepan of boiling water until just tender, following the directions on the package. Drain the noodles immediately and remove them to a bowl.

3 Toss the hot noodles with the dressing and the green onions. Top with the bean sprouts, cucumber and sesame seeds and serve.

— COOK'S TIP —

Soba are Japanese thin, brownish noodles made from buckwheat flour. They are available at Japanese markets.

Pork and Rice Vermicelli Salad

INGREDIENTS

Serves 4

8 ounces lean pork
2 garlic cloves, finely minced
2 slices fresh ginger, finely chopped
2–3 tablespoons rice wine
3 tablespoons vegetable oil
2 stalks lemongrass, finely chopped
2 teaspoons curry powder
6 ounces bean sprouts
8 ounces rice vermicelli, soaked in
   warm water until soft and drained
½ lettuce, finely shredded
2 tablespoons chopped fresh mint leaves
lemon juice and Asian fish sauce, to taste
salt and freshly ground black pepper
2 green onions, finely sliced, 1 ounce
   roasted peanuts, finely chopped, and
   pork cracklings (optional), to garnish

1 Cut the pork in strips and put in a dish with half the garlic and ginger. Pour on 2 tablespoons of the rice wine, season, stir and marinate for 1 hour.

2 Fry the rest of the garlic and ginger briefly. Stir in the pork and juices, lemongrass and curry. Fry until golden, adding rice wine if needed.

3 Place the bean sprouts in a sieve. Blanch them by lowering the sieve into a saucepan of boiling water for 1 minute, then drain and refresh under cold running water. Drain again. Using the same water, cook the rice vermicelli for 3–5 minutes until tender, drain and rinse under cold running water. Drain and transfer to a bowl.

4 Add the bean sprouts, lettuce and mint leaves and season with the lemon juice and fish sauce. Toss lightly.

5 Divide the noodle mixture among four serving plates, making a nest on each. Spoon the pork mixture on top. Garnish with green onions, peanuts and pork cracklings, if using.

Thai Chicken Salad

This is a superb main meal salad, and once you have prepared the various ingredients, it is simple to cook and assemble. Most of the Thai ingredients are available at Asian markets, but if you can't get roasted ground rice, see the Cook's Tip to make your own.

INGREDIENTS

Serves 4–6
1 pound ground chicken
1 stalk lemongrass, finely chopped
3 kaffir lime leaves, finely chopped
4 red chilies, seeded and chopped
4 tablespoons lime juice
2 tablespoons Asian fish sauce
1 tablespoon roasted ground rice
2 green onions, sliced
2 tablespoons cilantro leaves
mixed salad greens, cucumber and
    tomato slices, to serve
sprigs of mint, to garnish

— COOK'S TIP —

Use sticky, or glutinous, rice to make roasted ground rice. Put it in a frying pan and dry-roast until golden. Remove and grind to a powder with a mortar and pestle, food processor or blender. Store in a glass jar in a cool, dry place.

2 Stir constantly until cooked; this will take 7–10 minutes.

1 Heat a large non-stick frying pan. Add the ground chicken and cook in a little water.

3 Transfer the cooked chicken to a large bowl with all the remaining ingredients. Mix thoroughly.

4 Arrange the mixed salad greens, cucumber and sliced tomato on a large serving platter. Spoon the flavored chicken mixture on top of the salad and garnish with some sprigs of fresh mint.

Warm Duck Salad

The rich gamey flavor of duck provides the basis for this delicious salad. Serve it in late summer or autumn and enjoy the warm flavors of orange and coriander.

INGREDIENTS

Serves 4

1 small orange, cut into half slices
2 boneless duck breasts
¾ cup dry white wine
1 teaspoon ground coriander
½ teaspoon ground cumin
2 tablespoons superfine sugar
juice of ½ small lime or lemon
3 tablespoons olive oil
3 slices white bread, crusts removed
    and cut into fingers
½ head escarole lettuce
½ head frisée lettuce
2 tablespoons sunflower oil
4 sprigs fresh cilantro
salt and cayenne pepper

1 Place the orange slices in a small saucepan, cover with water and bring to a boil. Simmer for about 5 minutes, then drain and set aside.

2 Cut the skin of the duck breasts diagonally and rub with salt. Place a heavy frying pan over steady heat and cook the breasts for 20 minutes, turning once, until they are medium-rare. Transfer to a warm plate, cover and keep warm. Pour away any excess fat from the pan.

3 Heat the browned bits in the pan until they begin to caramelize. Stir in the wine, then add the coriander, cumin, sugar and orange slices. Boil until fairly thick, then add the lime juice. Season with salt and cayenne, then transfer to a bowl and keep warm.

4 Heat the olive oil in a frying pan and fry the bread until brown.

5 Toss the salad leaves in a little oil and arrange on four serving plates.

6 Slice the duck breasts diagonally and place on top of the salad. Spoon on the dressing, scatter with croutons, decorate with a sprig of cilantro and serve.

Salade Mouclade

This spectacular salad comes from La Rochelle in southwest France.

INGREDIENTS

Serves 4

3 tablespoons olive oil
1 onion, finely chopped
1¾ cups puy or green lentils, soaked for 2 hours
3¾ cups vegetable stock
4−4½ pounds fresh mussels in their shells
5 tablespoons white wine
½ teaspoon mild curry paste
1 pinch saffron
2 tablespoons heavy cream
2 large carrots
4 celery stalks
1 tablespoon olive oil
2 pounds young spinach, washed and stems removed
salt and cayenne pepper

1 Heat the olive oil in a heavy saucepan and fry the chopped onion for 6−8 minutes. Add the drained lentils and stock, bring to a boil and simmer for 45 minutes. Remove from the heat and cool.

2 Clean the mussels thoroughly, discarding any that are damaged or do not close when sharply tapped. Place in a large saucepan, add the wine, cover and steam over high heat for 12 minutes. Strain the mussels in a colander, collecting the cooking liquid in a bowl; discard any mussels that have not opened. Cool, then take them out of their shells.

3 Strain the mussel liquid through a fine sieve into a small frying pan. Stir in the curry paste and saffron, then cook over high heat until almost dry. Remove from the heat and stir in the heavy cream. Season and combine with the mussels.

4 Bring a saucepan of salted water to a boil. Cut the carrots and celery into 2-inch matchsticks, cook for 3 minutes, drain, cool and moisten with olive oil.

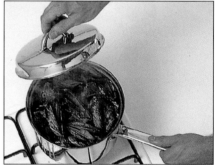

5 Place the spinach in a large pan, cover and steam for 2−3 minutes. Immerse in cold water and press the leaves dry in a colander with the back of a large spoon. Moisten with olive oil, season and set aside.

6 Spoon the lentils into the center of four serving plates. Place five leaves of spinach around the edge of each one and garnish with the carrot and celery. Spoon the mussels over the lentils and serve at room temperature.

Curly Endive Salad with Bacon

This country-style salad is popular all over France. When they are in season, dandelion leaves often replace the endive and the salad is sometimes sprinkled with chopped hard-cooked egg.

INGREDIENTS

Serves 4

8 ounces curly endive or escarole leaves
5–6 tablespoons extra virgin olive oil
6-ounce piece of smoked bacon, diced, or 6 pieces smoked bacon, cut crosswise into thin strips
2 slices white bread, cubed
1 small garlic clove, finely chopped
1 tablespoon red wine vinegar
2 teaspoons Dijon mustard
salt and freshly ground black pepper

1 Tear the endive into bite-size pieces and put them in a salad bowl.

COOK'S TIP

Use frisée or escarole leaves as soon as possible after purchase. To store, wrap the leaves and place in the salad drawer of the fridge for up to three days.

2 Heat 1 tablespoon of the oil in a frying pan over medium-low heat and add the bacon. Fry until browned, stirring occasionally. Remove with a slotted spoon and drain on paper towels.

3 Add 2 tablespoons of oil to the pan and fry the bread cubes over medium-high heat, turning frequently, until evenly browned. Remove with a slotted spoon and drain on paper towels. Wipe the pan clean.

4 Stir the garlic, vinegar and mustard into the pan with the remaining oil and heat until just warm, whisking to combine. Season to taste, then pour over the salad and sprinkle with the fried bacon and croutons.

Goat Cheese Salad

INGREDIENTS

Serves 4

2 tablespoons olive oil
4 slices French bread, ½ inch thick
8 ounces mixed salad greens, torn in
  small pieces
4 rounds firm goat cheese, about
  2 ounces each, rind removed
1 yellow or red bell pepper, seeded
  and finely diced
1 small red onion, thinly sliced
3 tablespoons chopped fresh parsley
2 tablespoons snipped fresh chives

For the dressing

2 tablespoons wine vinegar
1 teaspoon wholegrain mustard
5 tablespoons olive oil
salt and freshly ground black pepper

COOK'S TIP

For a substantial salad, use more salad greens
and make double the dressing. Add
4 ounces sliced cooked green beans to the
leaves, and toss with half the dressing. Top
with the cheeses and remaining dressing.

1 To make the dressing, mix the
vinegar and salt with a fork until
dissolved. Stir in the mustard.
Gradually stir in the oil until blended.
Season with pepper and set aside.
Preheat the broiler.

2 Heat the oil in a frying pan. When
hot, add the bread and cook for
1 minute until golden. Turn and cook
the other side for 30 seconds more.
Drain on paper towels and set aside.

3 Place the salad greens in a bowl.
Add 3 tablespoons of the dressing
and toss to coat. Divide the dressed
leaves among four salad plates.

4 Put the goat cheese rounds, cut
side up, on a baking sheet and
broil for 1–2 minutes until golden.

5 Place one goat cheese round in
the center of each plate. Scatter
the diced pepper, red onion, parsley
and chives over the salad. Drizzle with
the remaining dressing and serve.

Warm Chicken Liver Salad

This popular salad makes an excellent light lunch or summer evening meal. For a more substantial meal, you could fry 3–4 pieces of bacon, crumble it and toss it in with the salad at the end.

INGREDIENTS

Serves 4

4 ounces each fresh young spinach
   leaves, arugula and lollo rosso lettuce
2 pink grapefruit
6 tablespoons sunflower oil
2 teaspoons sesame oil
2 teaspoons soy sauce
8 ounces chicken livers, chopped
salt and freshly ground black pepper

1 Wash, dry and tear up all the spinach and salad greens. Mix them well in a large salad bowl.

2 Cut away the peel and white pith from the grapefruit, then segment them, catching the juice in a bowl. Add the segments to the greens in the bowl.

3 Mix 4 tablespoons of the sunflower oil with the sesame oil, soy sauce, seasoning and grapefruit juice to taste.

4 Heat the rest of the sunflower oil in a small pan and cook the liver for 4–5 minutes until firm and lightly browned, stirring occasionally.

5 Pour the chicken livers and dressing over the salad and serve at once.

--- COOK'S TIP ---

Chicken or turkey livers are often sold frozen. They are ideal for this recipe, and there's no need to defrost them completely before cooking.

Pasta Salad with Broccoli and Artichokes

INGREDIENTS

Serves 4

7 tablespoons olive oil
1 red bell pepper, quartered, seeded and thinly sliced
1 onion, halved and thinly sliced
1 teaspoon dried thyme
3 tablespoons sherry vinegar
1 pound pasta shapes, such as penne or fusilli
2 jars (6 ounces each) marinated artichoke hearts, drained and thinly sliced
5 ounces cooked broccoli, chopped
20–25 black olives, pitted and chopped
2 tablespoons chopped fresh parsley
salt and freshly ground black pepper

1 Heat 2 tablespoons of the oil in a non-stick frying pan. Add the bell pepper and onion and cook over low heat for 8–10 minutes, until just soft, stirring occasionally.

2 Stir in the thyme, salt and vinegar. Cook for 30 seconds longer, stirring, then set aside.

3 Bring a large pan of salted water to a boil. Add the pasta and cook until just tender (see package instructions for timing). Drain, rinse with hot water, then drain again well. Transfer to a large bowl. Add 2 tablespoons of the oil and toss well to coat.

4 Add the artichokes, broccoli, olives, parsley, pepper and onion mixture and remaining oil to the pasta. Season with salt and pepper and stir to mix. Let stand at least 1 hour before serving, or chill overnight.

Spinach and Mushroom Salad

This is an excellent choice for anyone counting calories as it is very low in fat, yet still tasty, with a variety of flavors and textures.

INGREDIENTS

Serves 2–3
10 ears of baby corn
4 ounces mushrooms
2 tomatoes
1 small onion
20 small spinach leaves
1 ounce watercress
salt and freshly ground black pepper
2 sprigs fresh cilantro, to garnish

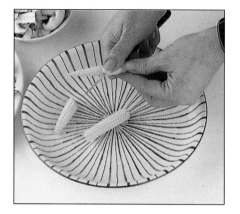

1 Halve the baby corn, and slice the mushrooms and tomatoes. Cut the onion into very thin rings.

2 Toss the spinach, baby corn, onion, mushrooms, tomatoes and watercress together and arrange on a serving plate. Season with salt and pepper and garnish with fresh cilantro and lime slices.

Nutty Bean and Pasta Salad

INGREDIENTS

Serves 4
1 onion, thinly sliced
½ cup canned kidney beans, drained and rinsed
1 zucchini, sliced
1 summer squash, sliced
2 ounces pasta shells, cooked
½ cup cashews
¼ cup peanuts

For the dressing
½ cup sour cream
2 tablespoons plain low-fat yogurt
1 fresh green chili, seeded and finely chopped
1 tablespoon chopped fresh cilantro
½ teaspoon salt
½ teaspoon freshly ground black pepper
½ teaspoon crushed dried red chilies
1 tablespoon lemon juice
lime wedges, to garnish

1 Arrange the onion rings, kidney beans, zucchini slices and pasta in a salad dish and sprinkle with the cashews and peanuts.

2 Make the dressing in a separate bowl: blend the sour cream, yogurt, green chili, fresh cilantro and salt and beat well using a fork.

3 Sprinkle the black pepper, crushed red chilies and lemon juice over the dressing. Garnish the salad with the lime wedges and serve with the dressing in a separate bowl or poured over the salad.

VARIATION

Instead of red kidney beans, add a mixture of beans such as chick-peas, cannellini beans and black-eyed peas. Add sliced cucumber rather than zucchini and vary the pasta shapes and nuts.

Mexican Mixed Salad

Ingredients

Serves 4

3 tablespoons white wine vinegar
1 teaspoon Dijon mustard
2 tablespoons cream
³/₄ cup vegetable oil, plus extra for
    frying
1 small garlic clove, finely chopped
1 teaspoon ground cumin
1 teaspoon dried oregano
1 pound lean ground beef
1 small onion, chopped
¹/₄ teaspoon cayenne pepper
1 can (7 ounces) corn, drained
1 can (15 ounces) kidney beans, drained
1 tablespoon chopped fresh cilantro,
    plus extra cilantro leaves, to garnish
1 small head romaine lettuce
3 tomatoes, sliced
2 cups grated Cheddar cheese
1 avocado
2 ounces black olives, pitted and sliced
4 green onions, thinly sliced
salt and freshly ground black pepper
tortilla chips, to serve

1 To make the dressing, mix the vinegar and salt with a fork until dissolved. Stir in the mustard and cream. Gradually stir in the oil until blended, then add the garlic, cumin, oregano and pepper and set aside.

2 Heat 2 tablespoons vegetable oil in a large frying pan. Add the beef, onion, salt and cayenne and cook for 5–7 minutes, until just browned. Stir frequently to break up any lumps. Drain and let cool.

3 Toss the beef mixture, corn, kidney beans and cilantro.

4 Stack the lettuce leaves on top of each other and shred them finely. Place in another bowl and toss with 3 tablespoons of the dressing. Place the lettuce on four serving plates.

5 Mound the meat mixture in the center. Arrange the tomatoes at the edges and sprinkle with the cheese.

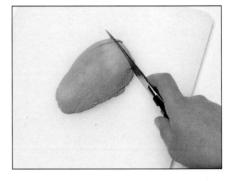

6 Halve, pit, peel and dice the avocado and add to salad. Scatter the olives and green onions on top. Pour the remaining dressing over the salad and garnish with cilantro. Serve with tortilla chips.

Thai Beef Salad

A hearty salad of beef, laced with a chili and lime dressing.

INGREDIENTS

Serves 4

2 sirloin steaks, 8 ounces each
1 red onion, finely sliced
½ cucumber, finely sliced into
    matchsticks
1 stalk lemongrass, finely chopped
juice of 2 limes
1–2 tablespoons Asian fish sauce
2 tablespoons chopped green onions
2–4 red chilies, seeded and finely
    sliced, fresh cilantro, Chinese
    mustard greens and mint leaves, to
    garnish

1 Pan-fry or grill the beef steaks to medium-rare. Allow to rest for 10–15 minutes.

2 When cool, use a sharp knife to slice the beef steaks thinly. Put the slices in a large bowl.

3 Add the sliced onion, cucumber matchsticks and lemongrass.

4 Add the green onions. Toss and season with lime juice and fish sauce. Serve at room temperature or chilled, garnished with the chilies, cilantro, mustard greens and mint.

Classic Salads

Many countries have their favorite salads. Some are specialties of
particular regions, while others are "invented" by chefs for their clientele
and become associated with towns, villages, or a restaurant or hotel.
As their popularity spreads, these salads earn the title "Classic Salads,"
and today there are many such examples. Indonesia's Gado-Gado is a
feast for the eyes and the palate and is deservedly world renowned.
Salade Niçoise from Provence, with its delicious combination of tuna,
olives, beans and tomatoes, is another of the best-known classic salads.
Lebanese Tabbouleh mixes bulgur wheat with onions, parsley and mint,
and Caesar Salad, one of the most famous salads of all, has a classic
dressing of egg, olive oil, lemon juice and anchovies.

Salade Niçoise

INGREDIENTS

Serves 4

6 tablespoons olive oil
½ tablespoon tarragon vinegar
1 teaspoon tarragon or Dijon mustard
1 small garlic clove, crushed
4 ounces green beans
12 small new potatoes
3–4 Bibb lettuces, roughly chopped
1 can (7 ounces) tuna in oil, drained
6 anchovy fillets, halved lengthwise
12 black olives, pitted
4 tomatoes, chopped
4 green onions, finely chopped
2 teaspoons capers
2 tablespoons pine nuts
2 hard-cooked eggs, chopped
salt and freshly ground black pepper
crusty bread, to serve

1 Mix the oil, vinegar, mustard, garlic and seasoning with a wooden spoon in a large salad bowl.

COOK'S TIP

Look for waxy salad potatoes such as Ratte, Belle de Fontenay or Yukon Gold.

2 Cook the green beans and potatoes in separate pans of boiling salted water until just tender. Drain and add to the bowl with the lettuce, tuna, anchovies, olives, tomatoes, green onions and capers.

3 Just before serving, toast the pine nuts in a small frying pan until lightly browned.

4 Sprinkle the pine nuts over the salad while still hot, add the eggs and toss all the ingredients together well. Serve with crusty bread.

Caesar Salad

For this famous salad, created by the Tijuanan chef called Caesar Cardini in the 1920s, the dressing is traditionally tossed into crunchy romaine lettuce, but any crisp lettuce will do.

INGREDIENTS

Serves 4
1 large head romaine lettuce
4 thick slices white or whole wheat
   bread without crusts, cubed
3 tablespoons olive oil
1 garlic clove, crushed

For the dressing
1 egg
1 garlic clove, minced
2 tablespoons lemon juice
dash of Worcestershire sauce
3 anchovy fillets, chopped
½ cup olive oil
5 tablespoons grated Parmesan cheese
salt and freshly ground black pepper

1 Preheat the oven to 425°F. Separate, rinse and dry the lettuce leaves. Tear the outer leaves roughly and chop the heart. Arrange the lettuce in a large salad bowl.

2 Mix together the cubed bread, olive oil and garlic in a separate bowl until the bread has soaked up the flavored oil. Lay the bread cubes on a baking sheet and place in the oven for 6–8 minutes (keeping an eye on them) until golden brown. Remove and let cool.

3 To make the dressing, break the egg into the bowl of a food processor or blender and add the garlic, lemon juice, Worcestershire sauce and one of the anchovy fillets. Blend until smooth.

4 With the motor running, pour in the olive oil in a thin stream until the dressing has the consistency of cream. Season with black pepper and a little salt if needed.

5 Pour the dressing over the salad greens and toss well, then toss in the garlic croutons, Parmesan cheese and the remaining anchovies and serve.

Tabbouleh

This classic Lebanese salad has become very popular in other countries. It makes an ideal substitute for a rich dish on a buffet table and is excellent served with cold sliced lamb.

INGREDIENTS

Serves 4

1 cup bulgur wheat
juice of 1 lemon
3 tablespoons olive oil
1½ ounces finely chopped fresh parsley
3 tablespoons chopped fresh mint
4–5 green onions, chopped
1 green bell pepper, seeded and sliced
salt and freshly ground black pepper
2 large tomatoes, diced, and a few
   black olives, pitted, to garnish

1 Put the bulgur wheat in a bowl. Add enough cold water to cover the wheat and let it stand for at least 30 minutes and up to 2 hours.

2 Drain and squeeze with your hands to remove excess water. The bulgur wheat will swell to double the size. (Spread on paper towels to dry the bulgur wheat completely.)

3 Place the bulgur wheat in a large bowl, add the lemon juice, oil and a little salt and pepper. Allow to stand for 1–2 hours if possible, in order for the flavors to develop.

4 Add the chopped parsley, mint, green onions and pepper and mix well. Garnish with diced tomatoes and olives and serve.

Yogurt with Cucumber

INGREDIENTS

Serves 4–6

½ cucumber
1 small onion
2 garlic cloves
1–2 sprigs fresh parsley
2 cups plain yogurt
¼ teaspoon paprika
salt and white pepper
fresh mint leaves, to garnish
pita bread (optional), to serve

1 Finely chop the cucumber and onion, crush the garlic and finely chop the parsley.

> — COOK'S TIP —
>
> They're not traditional, but other fresh herbs, such as mint or chives, would be equally good in this dish.

2 Lightly beat the yogurt and then add the cucumber, onion, garlic and parsley and season with salt and pepper to taste.

3 Sprinkle with a little paprika and chill for at least 1 hour. Garnish with mint leaves and serve with warm pita bread or as an accompaniment to meat, poultry and rice dishes.

New Potato and Chive Salad

The secret of a good potato salad is to mix the potatoes with the dressing while they are still warm so that they absorb the flavor.

INGREDIENTS

Serves 4–6
1½ pounds new potatoes (unpeeled)
4 green onions
3 tablespoons olive oil
1 tablespoon white wine vinegar
¾ teaspoon Dijon mustard
¾ cup mayonnaise
3 tablespoons snipped fresh chives
salt and freshly ground black pepper

1 Cook the potatoes in boiling salted water until tender. Meanwhile, finely chop the white parts of the green onions along with a little of the green part set aside.

2 Whisk together the oil, vinegar and mustard. Drain the potatoes well, then immediately toss lightly with the vinegar mixture and green onions and let cool.

3 Stir the mayonnaise and chives into the potatoes with salt and pepper to taste. Chill well until ready to serve with grilled sausages, roasted chicken or cold meats.

—— COOK'S TIP ——

Be on the lookout for small, waxy potatoes for salads and cold dishes – they are particularly good in this recipe.

Gado-Gado

Gado–Gado is a deservedly-famous classic salad from Indonesia. It features a colorful variety of cooked and raw ingredients. Tamarind pulp is easy to find in Asian markets.

INGREDIENTS

Serves 6
2 unripe pears
1–2 apples
juice of ½ lemon
banana leaf or lettuce leaves
1 small head romaine lettuce, shredded
½ cucumber, seeded, sliced and salted, set aside for 15 minutes, then rinsed and drained
6 small tomatoes, cut in wedges
3 slices fresh pineapple, cored and cut in wedges
3 eggs or 12 quail eggs, hard-cooked
6 ounces egg noodles, cooked, cooled and chopped
deep-fried onions, for garnish

For the peanut sauce
2–4 fresh red chilies, seeded and ground, or 1 tablespoon chili sambal
1¼ cups coconut milk
12 ounces crunchy peanut butter
1 tablespoon dark soy sauce or dark brown sugar
1 teaspoon tamarind pulp, soaked in 3 tablespoons warm water, strained and juice reserved
coarsely crushed peanuts
salt

1 To make the peanut sauce, put the chilies or chili sambal and coconut milk in a pan. Add the peanut butter and heat gently, stirring, until no lumps of peanut butter remain.

2 Allow to simmer gently until the sauce thickens, then add the soy sauce or sugar and tamarind juice. Season with salt to taste. Pour into a bowl and sprinkle with a few coarsely crushed peanuts.

3 Cut the unripe pears into matchsticks and slice the apples finely. Sprinkle all the fruit with lemon juice. Place the banana leaf or lettuce leaves on a flat platter and arrange the salad and fruit attractively on the top.

4 Slice or quarter the hard-cooked eggs (leave quail's eggs whole) and add to the salad with the chopped noodles and deep-fried onions.

5 Serve immediately, accompanied by a bowl of the peanut sauce.

Melon and Crab Salad

INGREDIENTS

Serves 6

1 pound fresh crabmeat
½ cup mayonnaise
3 tablespoons sour cream or plain
    yogurt
2 tablespoons olive oil
2 tablespoons lemon or lime juice
2–3 green onions, finely chopped
2 tablespoons finely chopped fresh
    cilantro
¼ teaspoon cayenne pepper
1½ cantaloupe or small honeydew
    melons
3 Belgian endives
salt and freshly ground black pepper
fresh cilantro sprigs, to garnish

1 Pick over the crabmeat very
carefully, removing any bits of shell
or cartilage. Leave the pieces of
crabmeat as large as possible.

2 In a medium-size mixing bowl,
combine all the other ingredients
except the melons and the endive
leaves and season to taste. Mix
everything well, then fold in the
crabmeat and mix carefully.

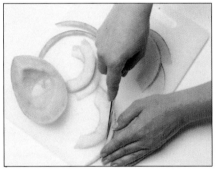

3 Halve the cantaloupes or melons
and remove and discard all the
seeds. Cut the melons into thin slices,
then remove the rind.

4 Arrange the salad on six individual
serving plates, making a decorative
design with the melon slices and the
endive leaves. Place a scoop of crab
salad on each serving plate and garnish
with fresh sprigs of cilantro.

Mixed Lettuce and Herb Salad

This classic salad is a good accompaniment for many dishes. It would be perfect served with most fish recipes, and it makes a refreshing side dish when served with roast meat.

INGREDIENTS

Serves 4
½ cucumber
mixed lettuce leaves
1 bunch watercress, about 4 ounces
1 Belgian endive
3 tablespoons mixed chopped fresh
   herbs such as parsley, thyme,
   tarragon, chives and chervil

For the dressing
1 tablespoon white wine vinegar
1 teaspoon mustard
5 tablespoons olive oil
salt and freshly ground black pepper

——— COOK'S TIP ———

Never dress a salad until just before serving as the lettuce leaves will wilt and become unpleasantly soggy if allowed to sit in dressing for too long.

1 To make the dressing, mix the vinegar and mustard together, then whisk in the oil and seasoning.

2 Peel the cucumber, if desired, then halve the cucumber lengthwise and scoop out the seeds. Thinly slice the cucumber. Tear the lettuce leaves into bite-size pieces.

3 Either toss the cucumber, lettuce, watercress, endive and herbs together in a bowl, or arrange them in the bowl in layers.

4 Stir the dressing, then pour it all over the salad, tossing it lightly to coat the salad ingredients. Serve immediately.

Turkish Feta Salad

This popular salad makes an excellent light lunch. The saltiness of the cheese is balanced by the refreshing salad vegetables.

INGREDIENTS

Serves 4
1 small head romaine lettuce
1 green bell pepper, seeded
1 red bell pepper, seeded
½ cucumber
4 tomatoes
1 red onion
2 cups crumbled feta cheese
black olives, pitted, to garnish

For the dressing
3 tablespoons olive oil
3 tablespoons lemon juice
1 garlic clove, crushed
1 tablespoon chopped fresh parsley
1 tablespoon chopped fresh mint
salt and freshly ground black pepper

1 Chop the lettuce into bite-size pieces. Seed the peppers, remove the cores and cut the flesh into thin strips. Chop the cucumber and slice or chop the tomatoes. Cut the onion in half, then slice finely.

2 Place the chopped lettuce, peppers, cucumber, tomatoes and onion in a large bowl. Scatter the feta over the top and toss together lightly.

3 To make the dressing for the salad, blend together the olive oil, lemon juice and crushed garlic in a small bowl. Stir in the chopped fresh parsley and mint and season with a little salt and pepper, to taste.

4 Carefully pour the fresh dressing over the salad in the bowl, toss lightly and serve garnished with a handful of black olives.

Persian Cucumber Salad

This simple classic salad can be served with just about any dish – don't add the dressing until just before you are ready to serve.

INGREDIENTS

Serves 4
4 tomatoes
½ cucumber
1 onion
1 small head romaine lettuce

For the dressing
2 tablespoons olive oil
juice of 1 lemon
1 garlic clove, crushed
salt and freshly ground black pepper

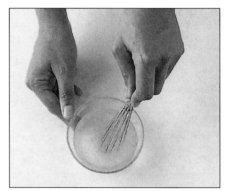

1 Cut the tomatoes and cucumber into small cubes. Finely chop the onion and tear the lettuce into pieces.

2 Place the tomatoes, cucumber, onion and lettuce in a large salad bowl and mix lightly together.

3 To make the dressing, pour the olive oil into a small bowl. Add the lemon juice, garlic and seasoning and blend together well. Pour on top of the salad and toss lightly to mix. Sprinkle with black pepper and serve with meat or rice dishes.

SIDE SALADS

In France, side salads are often served separately from the main course, partly to refresh the palate, and partly, no doubt, so that the diner can appreciate the individual tastes and textures of the salad. Elsewhere, salads are served alongside the main course, either in individual salad plates or in a large salad bowl. Whichever you prefer, a side salad makes a very good accompaniment to any main course. Leafy salads, like Citrus Green Leaf Salad with Croutons, are excellent with almost any dish, but are particularly popular with pizzas and pasta dishes. Other side salads can feature a range of colorful vegetables — Roasted Pepper Salad looks and tastes wonderful and is lovely as part of a buffet, or with fish or poultry.

Coleslaw with Dates and Apples

Three types of cabbage are shredded together for serving raw, so that the maximum amount of vitamin C is retained, making this a crunchy as well as a nutritious salad.

INGREDIENTS

Serves 6–8
¼ small green cabbage, shredded
¼ small red cabbage, shredded
¼ small savoy cabbage, shredded
1 cup dried pitted dates
3 Granny Smith apples
juice of 1 lemon
2 teaspoons caraway seeds

For the dressing
4 tablespoons olive oil
1 tablespoon cider vinegar
1 teaspoon honey
salt and freshly ground black pepper

1 Finely shred all the cabbages and place them in a large salad bowl.

2 Chop the dates and add them to the cabbage.

3 Core the apples, and slice them thinly into a mixing bowl. Add the lemon juice and toss together to prevent discoloration before adding to the salad bowl.

4 To make the dressing, combine the oil, vinegar and honey in a screw-top jar. Add salt and pepper, close the jar tightly and shake well. Pour the dressing over the salad, toss lightly, then sprinkle with the caraway seeds and toss again.

--- VARIATION ---

The dried dates in this dish give the salad a faintly Middle Eastern flavor. You could emphasize this flavor by substituting 1–1½ ounces pine nuts for the caraway seeds. Dry-fry them briefly until golden and then sprinkle over the salad before serving.

Sprouted Seed Salad

Bean sprouts make a perfect salad ingredient, adding their unique texture and flavor.

INGREDIENTS

Serves 4
2 Granny Smith apples
4 ounces alfalfa sprouts
4 ounces bean sprouts
4 ounces aduki bean sprouts
¼ cucumber, sliced
1 bunch watercress, trimmed
1 carton mustard sprouts and
    watercress, trimmed

For the dressing
¾ cup low-fat plain yogurt
juice of ½ lemon
bunch of chives, snipped
2 tablespoons chopped fresh herbs
ground black pepper

1 Core and slice the apples and mix with the other salad ingredients.

2 Shake together the dressing ingredients in a jar. Drizzle over the salad and toss just before serving.

--- COOK'S TIP ---

You can sprout the beans at home to ensure that they are really fresh. Always buy the beans at a health-food store and ask for those that are selected for sprouting.

Eggplant Salad

This interesting and unusual salad comes from Thailand.

INGREDIENTS

Serves 4–6

2 eggplant
1 tablespoon vegetable oil
2 tablespoons dried shrimp, soaked and drained
1 tablespoon coarsely chopped garlic
1 hard-cooked egg, shelled and chopped
4 shallots, finely sliced into rings
fresh cilantro leaves and 2 red chilies, seeded and sliced, to garnish

For the dressing

2 tablespoons lime juice
1 teaspoon sugar
1/2 tablespoon Asian fish sauce

1 Grill or roast the eggplant until charred and tender.

2 When cool enough to handle, peel away the skin and slice the flesh.

COOK'S TIP

For an interesting variation, try using salted duck or quail eggs, cut in half, instead of chopped hen eggs.

3 Heat the oil in a small frying pan, add the drained shrimp and garlic and fry until golden. Remove from the pan and set aside.

4 To make the dressing, put the lime juice, sugar and fish sauce in a small bowl and whisk together until well blended.

5 To serve, arrange the sliced eggplant on a serving dish. Sprinkle with the chopped egg, shallots and shrimp mixture. Drizzle with the dressing and garnish with cilantro and red chilies.

Peppery Bean Salad

INGREDIENTS

Serves 4–6

1 can (15 ounces) kidney beans
1 can (15 ounces) black-eyed peas
1 can (15 ounces) chick-peas
¼ red bell pepper
¼ green bell pepper
6 radishes
1 tablespoon chopped green onion
1 teaspoon ground cumin
1 tablespoon ketchup
½ tablespoon olive oil
1 tablespoon white wine vinegar
1 garlic clove, crushed
½ teaspoon hot pepper sauce
salt
sliced green onion, to garnish

1 Drain the canned beans and peas and rinse under cold running water. Shake off the excess water and pour them into a large salad bowl.

2 Core, seed and chop the peppers. Trim the radishes and slice thinly. Add to the beans with the pepper and green onion.

3 Combine the cumin, ketchup, oil, vinegar and garlic in a small bowl. Add a little salt and hot pepper sauce to taste and stir again thoroughly.

4 Pour the dressing over the salad and mix. Chill for at least 1 hour before serving, garnished with sliced green onion.

—————— COOK'S TIP ——————

For an even tastier salad, allow the ingredients to marinate for a few hours.

Yogurt Salad

A delicious salad with a yogurt base, this is really an Eastern version of coleslaw. For a low-calorie dish, use low-fat yogurt.

INGREDIENTS

Serves 3–4

1½ cups plain yogurt
2 teaspoons honey
2 carrots, thickly sliced
2 green onions, coarsely chopped
4 ounces cabbage, finely shredded
¾ cup golden raisins
½ cup cashews
16 green grapes, halved
½ teaspoon salt
1 teaspoon chopped fresh mint
3–4 mint sprigs (optional), to garnish

1 Using a fork, beat the yogurt in a bowl with the clear honey.

2 Combine the carrots, green onions, cabbage, raisins, cashews, grapes, salt and chopped mint.

3 Pour the yogurt mixture over the salad ingredients and lightly toss together to mix.

4 Either chill the salad in the fridge for several hours or until required, or transfer to a large serving dish and serve immediately. Garnish the salad with fresh mint sprigs, if desired.

—— COOK'S TIP ——

Serve this salad with kebabs or other barbecued meat or fish. It is also delicious as part of a buffet meal, served with other Middle Eastern appetizers, like dolmades, fried eggplant or falafel.

Spicy Baby Vegetable Salad

This warm vegetable salad makes an excellent accompaniment to almost any main course dish.

INGREDIENTS

Serves 6

10 small new potatoes, halved
15 baby carrots
10 baby zucchini
1½ cups button mushrooms

For the dressing

3 tablespoons lemon juice
1½ tablespoons olive oil
1 tablespoon chopped fresh cilantro
2 small green chilies, seeded and finely chopped
1 teaspoon salt

1 Wash and boil the potatoes and carrots until tender. Trim the zucchini and steam until tender. Drain all the vegetables and place in a large serving dish.

2 In a separate bowl, mix together the lemon juice, olive oil, chopped cilantro, green chilies and salt until well blended.

3 Pour the dressing over the vegetables and toss to mix. Serve with grilled meat or fish.

Pepper, Cucumber and Tomato Salad

This simple, refreshing peasant salad is a popular dish all over the Middle East.

INGREDIENTS

Serves 4

1 yellow or red bell pepper
1 large cucumber
4–5 tomatoes
1 bunch green onions
2 tablespoons finely chopped fresh
    parsley
2 tablespoons finely chopped fresh mint
2 tablespoons finely chopped fresh
    cilantro
2 garlic cloves, crushed
5 tablespoons olive oil
juice of 2 lemons
salt and freshly ground black pepper
2 pita breads, to serve

1 Slice the pepper, discarding the seeds and core, then roughly chop the cucumber and tomatoes. Place them in a large salad bowl.

2 Trim and slice the green onions. Add to the cucumber, tomatoes and pepper with the finely chopped parsley, mint and cilantro.

3 To make the dressing, blend the garlic with the olive oil and lemon juice in a cup, then season to taste with salt and black pepper. Pour the dressing over the salad and toss lightly to mix.

4 Toast the pita bread in a toaster or under a hot broiler until crisp and then serve it alongside the salad.

VARIATION

If you prefer, make this salad in the traditional way. After toasting the pita bread until crisp, crush it in your hand and then sprinkle it over the salad before serving. Alternatively, cut the pita bread in half and open up to make pockets. Spoon the salad into the pockets for a Middle Eastern sandwich.

COOK'S TIP

Although the recipe calls for only 2 tablespoons of each of the herbs, if you have plenty on hand, then you can add as much as you like to this aromatic salad.

Watercress and Potato Salad

New potatoes are equally good hot or cold, and this colorful, nutritious salad is an ideal way of making the most of them.

INGREDIENTS

Serves 4

1 pound small new potatoes, unpeeled
1 bunch watercress
1½ cups cherry tomatoes, halved
2 tablespoons pumpkin seeds
3 tablespoons low-fat sour cream
1 tablespoon cider vinegar
1 teaspoon brown sugar
salt and paprika

1 Cook the potatoes in lightly salted, boiling water until just tender, then drain and let cool.

2 Toss together the potatoes, watercress, tomatoes, and pumpkin seeds in a bowl.

3 Place the sour cream, vinegar, sugar, salt, and paprika in a screw-top jar and shake well to mix. Pour over the salad just before serving.

VARIATION

To make Spinach and Potato Salad, substitute 1 bunch baby spinach leaves, trimmed, for the watercress.

COOK'S TIP

If you are preparing this salad in advance, mix the dressing in the jar and add it just before serving.

Beet, Chicory and Orange Salad

A refreshing salad that goes well with grilled meats or fish. Alternatively, arrange it prettily on individual plates and serve as a summer starter.

INGREDIENTS

Serves 4

2 cooked beets, diced
2 Belgian endive, sliced
1 large orange
4 tablespoons low-fat plain yogurt
2 teaspoons wholegrain mustard
salt and freshly ground black pepper

COOK'S TIP

If you prefer, use a selection of leaves instead of just endive. Choose slightly bitter leaves such as escarole, along with strongly flavored leaves like arugula or spinach. Tear the leaves into pieces before mixing with the beets.

1 Mix together the diced, cooked beets and endive in a large serving bowl.

2 Finely grate the zest from the orange. With a sharp knife, remove all the peel and white pith. Cut out the segments, catching the juice in a bowl and add the segments to the salad.

3 Add the orange zest, yogurt, mustard, and seasoning to the orange juice, mix thoroughly, then spoon over the salad.

Roasted Pepper Salad

This colorful salad is very easy to make up to a day in advance, and the sharp-sweet dressing mingles with the mild pepper flavors.

INGREDIENTS

Serves 4

3 large red, green and yellow bell peppers, halved and seeded
4 ounces feta cheese, diced or crumbled
1 tablespoon sherry vinegar or red wine vinegar
1 tablespoon clear honey
salt and freshly ground black pepper

1 Arrange the pepper halves in a single layer, skin side up on a baking sheet. Place the peppers under a hot broiler until the skin is blackened and beginning to blister.

2 Place the peppers in a plastic bag and close the end. Leave until cool, then peel off and discard the skin.

3 Arrange the peppers on a platter and sprinkle with the cheese. Stir together the vinegar, honey, and seasoning, then sprinkle over the salad. Chill until ready to serve.

Thai Cabbage Salad

INGREDIENTS

Serves 4–6

2 tablespoons Asian fish sauce
grated rind of 1 lime
½ tablespoon lime juice
½ cup coconut milk
2 tablespoons vegetable oil
2 large red chilies, seeded and cut into
   thin strips
6 garlic cloves, finely minced
6 shallots, finely sliced
1 small cabbage, shredded
2 tablespoons coarsely chopped roasted
   peanuts, to serve

1 Make the dressing by combining the fish sauce, lime zest and juice and coconut milk. Set aside.

2 Heat the oil and stir-fry the chilies, garlic and shallots until the shallots are crisp. Transfer to a plate.

3 Blanch the cabbage in boiling salted water for 2–3 minutes, drain and place in a large bowl.

4 Stir the dressing into the cabbage. Mix well, then transfer into a serving dish. Sprinkle with the fried shallot mixture and the roasted peanuts.

COOK'S TIP

Other vegetables, such as broccoli, cauliflower and bean sprouts, can also be prepared in this way.

Green Bean Salad

You could make this lovely dish at any time of the year using imported or frozen vegetables and still get a pretty, healthy – and unusual – salad.

INGREDIENTS

Serves 4
6 ounces shelled fava beans
4 ounces green beans, quartered
4 ounces snow peas
8–10 small fresh mint leaves
3 green onions, chopped
4 tablespoons extra virgin olive oil
1 tablespoon cider vinegar
1 tablespoon chopped fresh mint, or
 1 teaspoon dried mint
1 garlic clove, crushed
salt and freshly ground black pepper

1 Plunge the fava beans into a saucepan of boiling water and bring back to a boil. Remove from the heat immediately and plunge into cold water. Drain. Repeat with the beans.

2 Mix together the blanched broad and green beans, the raw snow peas, fresh mint leaves and chopped green onions.

3 Blend the olive oil, vinegar, chopped mint, garlic and seasoning thoroughly, then pour over the salad and toss well. Chill until ready to serve.

Quick Ratatouille Salad

This salad is a delicious variation on the cooked dish. The key thing is that it keeps well – so well, in fact, it improves if eaten the next day.

INGREDIENTS

Serves 4

1 small eggplant
4 tablespoons olive oil
1 onion, sliced
1 green bell pepper, seeded and
    cut into strips
3 garlic cloves, crushed
1–2 tablespoons cider vinegar
8 tiny firm tomatoes, halved
salt and mixed ground peppercorns
sprigs of oregano, to garnish

1 Slice and quarter the eggplant. Place in a colander and sprinkle with plenty of salt. Let stand for 20 minutes, then drain off any liquid and rinse well under cold water.

2 Heat the oil in a large pan and gently sauté the onion, pepper and garlic, then stir in the eggplant and toss over high heat for 5 minutes.

3 When the eggplant is beginning to turn golden, add the cider vinegar, tomatoes and seasoning to taste. Let cool, then chill well. Season to taste again before serving, garnished with sprigs of oregano.

> — COOK'S TIP —
>
> Once the eggplants are rinsed, squeeze dry in sheets of paper towels – the drier they are, the quicker they will cook and brown.

Crisp Fruity Salad

Crisp lettuce, tangy cheese and crunchy pieces of fruit make a refreshing salad for any occasion.

INGREDIENTS

Serves 4

½ head romaine lettuce
3 ounces grapes, seeded and halved
½ cup sharp Cheddar cheese, grated
1 large Granny Smith apple, cored and
    thinly sliced
6–7 tablespoons mild French
    vinaigrette (see Cook's Tip)
3 tablespoons garlic croutons

1 Tear the lettuce leaves into small pieces and place in a salad bowl. Add the grapes, cheese and apple.

2 Pour the dressing over the salad. Toss well and serve immediately, sprinkled with garlic croutons.

> — COOK'S TIP —
>
> Mix 1 tablespoon French mustard, 1 tablespoon white wine vinegar, a pinch of sugar, and seasoning with 4 tablespoons sunflower oil.

Spicy Potato Salad

This tasty salad is quick to prepare, and makes a satisfying accompaniment to grilled or barbecued meat or fish.

INGREDIENTS

Serves 6

2 pounds potatoes, peeled
2 red bell peppers
2 celery stalks
1 shallot
2–3 green onions
1 green chili
1 garlic clove, crushed
2 teaspoons finely snipped fresh chives
2 teaspoons finely chopped fresh basil
1 teaspoon finely chopped fresh parsley
1 tablespoon light cream or half-and-half
2 tablespoons sour cream
1 tablespoon mayonnaise
1 teaspoon mild mustard
½ tablespoon sugar
snipped fresh chives, to garnish

1 Boil the potatoes until tender but still firm. Drain and cool, then cut into 1-inch cubes and place in a large salad bowl.

2 Halve the peppers, cut away and discard the core and seeds and cut into small pieces. Finely chop the celery, shallot and green onions and slice the chili very thinly, discarding the seeds. Add the vegetables to the potatoes, along with the garlic and chopped herbs.

3 Blend the cream, sour cream, mayonnaise, mustard and sugar in a small bowl, stirring until the mixture is well combined.

4 Pour the creamy dressing over the prepared potato and vegetable salad and stir gently to coat it evenly. Serve the salad garnished with fresh snipped chives.

Sweet Potato and Carrot Salad

This salad has a sweet-and-sour taste, and can be served warm as part of a meal or eaten in a larger portion as a main course.

INGREDIENTS

Serves 4

1 sweet potato
2 carrots, cut into thick diagonal slices
3 tomatoes
8–10 iceberg lettuce leaves
½ cup canned chick-peas, drained

For the dressing

1 tablespoon honey
6 tablespoons low-fat plain yogurt
½ teaspoon salt
1 teaspoon freshly ground black pepper

For the garnish

1 tablespoon walnuts
1 tablespoon golden raisins
1 small onion, cut into rings

1 Peel the sweet potato and roughly dice. Boil until soft but not mushy, cover the pan and set aside.

2 Boil the carrots for just a few minutes, making sure they remain crunchy. Add the carrots to the sweet potatoes. Drain the water from the sweet potatoes and carrots and place together in a bowl.

3 Slice the tops off the tomatoes, then scoop out and discard the seeds. Coarsely chop the flesh.

4 Line a glass bowl with the lettuce leaves. Combine the sweet potatoes, carrots, chick-peas and tomatoes and place in the bowl. Add the chick-peas and tomatoes to the sweet potatoes and carrots, mix well and then spoon into the salad bowl.

5 To make the dressing, blend together the honey, plain yogurt, salt and black pepper and beat well using a fork.

6 Garnish the salad with walnuts, golden raisins, and onions. Top with the dressing or serve it in a separate bowl, if desired.

COOK'S TIP

To skin the tomatoes, plunge them into boiling water. (Don't seed them before doing this.) Leave for 1 minute, then remove and make a small slit in the skin. The entire skin should then slip off. Halve or quarter, remove seeds and then chop.

Mixed Green Salad

Mesclun is a ready-mixed Provençal green salad composed of several kinds of salad leaves and herbs. A typical combination might include arugula, radicchio, mâche and curly endive with fresh herbs such as chervil, basil, parsley and tarragon.

INGREDIENTS

Serves 4–6
1 garlic clove, peeled
2 tablespoons red wine or sherry
   vinegar
1 teaspoon Dijon mustard (optional)
5–8 tablespoons extra virgin olive oil
7–8 ounces mesclun (mixed salad
   leaves) and herbs
salt and freshly ground black pepper

1 Rub a large salad bowl with the garlic clove and leave in the bowl.

2 Add the vinegar, salt and pepper and mustard, if using. Stir to mix the ingredients and dissolve the salt, then whisk in the oil slowly.

3 Remove the garlic clove and stir the vinaigrette to combine. Add the salad greens to the bowl and toss well. Serve the salad at once.

VARIATION

Mesclun always contains some pungent leaves. When dandelion leaves are in season, they are usually found in the mixture, so use them when available.

Apple and Celeriac Salad

INGREDIENTS

Serves 3–4
1 celeriac (about 1½ pounds), peeled
2–3 teaspoons lemon juice
1 teaspoon walnut oil (optional)
1 Granny Smith apple
3 tablespoons mayonnaise
2 teaspoons Dijon mustard
1 tablespoon chopped fresh parsley
salt and freshly ground black pepper

1 Shred the celeriac in a food processor or blender, or cut it into very thin julienne strips. Place it in a mixing bowl and sprinkle with the lemon juice and the walnut oil, if using. Stir well to mix.

2 Peel the apple, if desired, cut it into quarters and remove the core. Slice very thinly crosswise and toss with the celeriac.

3 Mix the mayonnaise, mustard and parsley with salt and pepper to taste. Stir into the celeriac mixture. Chill for several hours before serving.

Bulgur Wheat Salad with Oranges and Almonds

INGREDIENTS

Serves 4

1 small green bell pepper
1 cup bulgur wheat
2½ cups water
¼ cucumber, diced
½ cup chopped fresh mint
¾ cup toasted almonds
grated zest and juice of 1 lemon
2 seedless oranges
salt and freshly ground black pepper
mint sprigs, to garnish

1 Using a sharp vegetable knife, carefully core, halve and seed the green pepper. Then cut it into small cubes and set aside.

2 Place the bulgur wheat in a saucepan and add the water. Bring to a boil, lower the heat, cover and simmer for 10–15 minutes until tender. Alternatively, place the bulgur wheat in a heatproof bowl, pour in the boiling water and let soak for 30 minutes. Most, if not all, of the water should be absorbed; drain off any excess.

3 Toss the bulgur wheat with the cucumber, green pepper, mint and toasted almonds in a serving bowl. Add the grated lemon zest and juice.

4 Cut the rind from the oranges. Working over the bowl to catch the juice, cut the oranges into neat segments. Add to the bulgur mixture, with seasoning, and toss lightly. Garnish with the mint sprigs.

Fruity Brown Rice Salad

An Asian-style dressing gives this colorful rice salad extra piquancy. Whole grains like brown rice are unrefined, so they retain their natural fiber, vitamins and minerals.

INGREDIENTS

Serves 4–6

¾ cup brown rice
1 small red bell pepper, cored, seeded and diced
1 can (7 ounces) corn, drained
3 tablespoons golden raisins
1 can (8 ounces) pineapple chunks
1 tablespoon light soy sauce
1 tablespoon sunflower oil
1 tablespoon hazelnut oil
1 garlic clove, crushed
1 teaspoon finely chopped fresh root ginger
salt and freshly ground black pepper
4 green onions, sliced, to garnish

1 Cook the brown rice in a large saucepan of lightly salted boiling water for about 30 minutes, or until it is tender. Drain thoroughly and cool.

2 Pour the rice into a bowl and add the red pepper, corn and raisins. Drain the pineapple pieces, reserving the juice, add them to the rice mixture and toss lightly.

3 Pour the reserved pineapple juice into a clean screw-top jar. Add the soy sauce, sunflower and hazelnut oils, garlic and ginger. Season to taste with salt and pepper. Then close the jar tightly and shake well to combine.

4 Pour the dressing over the salad and toss well. Sprinkle the green onions over the top. The salad is delicious as part of a summer buffet or served with grilled meat or fish.

VARIATION

Try a mixture of brown rice and wild rice instead of just the brown rice. Cook the rice mixture for the recommended time.

Citrus Green Leaf Salad with Croutons

Croutons add a delicious crunch to leafy salads, while the kumquats or orange segments provide color, as well as a good helping of vitamin C.

Ingredients

Serves 4–6
4 kumquats or 2 seedless oranges
7 ounces mixed salad greens
4 slices of whole wheat bread, crusts removed
2–3 tablespoons pine nuts, lightly toasted

For the dressing
shredded rind of 1 lemon and 1 tablespoon juice
3 tablespoons olive oil
1 teaspoon whole-grain mustard
1 garlic clove, crushed

1 Thinly slice the kumquat, or peel and segment the oranges.

— Cook's Tip —

Although not so low-calorie, croutons are especially good fried. Make garlic oil by soaking 1 crushed garlic clove in 2–3 tablespoons olive or sunflower oil for about 1 hour. Strain the oil into a pan and then fry the croutons over brisk heat until golden.

---

2 Tear all the salad greens into bite-size pieces and place together in a large salad bowl.

3 Toast the bread on both sides and cut into cubes. Add to the salad leaves with the sliced kumquats or orange segments.

4 Shake all the dressing ingredients together in a jar. Pour over the salad just before serving and scatter the toasted pine nuts over the top.

Mixed Bean Salad with Tomato Dressing

All beans are a good source of vegetable protein and minerals.

Ingredients

Serves 4
4 ounces green beans
1 can (15 ounces) mixed beans, drained and rinsed
2 celery stalks, finely chopped
1 small onion, finely chopped
3 tomatoes, chopped
3 tablespoons chopped fresh parsley, to garnish

For the dressing
3 tablespoons olive oil
2 teaspoons red wine vinegar
1 garlic clove, crushed
1 tablespoon tomato chutney
salt and freshly ground black pepper

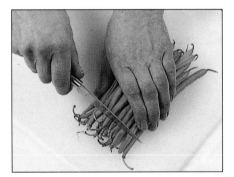

1 Remove the ends from the green beans, then cook the beans in boiling water for 5–6 minutes (or steam for 10 minutes) until tender. Drain, then refresh under cold running water and cut into thirds.

2 Place the green beans and mixed beans in a large bowl. Add the celery, onion and tomatoes and toss.

3 Shake the dressing ingredients together in a jar. Pour over the salad and sprinkle with the parsley.

— Cook's Tip —

Cans of mixed beans are a good way of quickly adding color and variety to a salad. They are normally made up of chick-peas, pinto, kidney, soy and aduki beans. Alternatively, you could choose a favorite bean for this salad. Pale green flageolets are very good. Always remember to rinse beans under cold running water before adding to a salad.

Feta and Bulgur in Radicchio Cups

The radicchio cups are an attractive way of serving this salad. Alternatively, spoon the bulgur wheat mixture onto a serving plate lined with romaine lettuce leaves.

INGREDIENTS

Serves 4
generous ³/₄ cup bulgur wheat
4 tablespoons olive oil
juice of 1 lemon, or more to taste
4 green onions, chopped
6 tablespoons chopped flat leaf parsley
3 tablespoons chopped fresh mint
2 tomatoes, peeled, seeded and diced
1½ cups feta cheese, cubed
salt and freshly ground black pepper
1 head radicchio, to serve
flat leaf parsley sprigs, to garnish

1 Soak the bulgur wheat in fresh cold water for 1 hour. Drain thoroughly in a sieve and press out the excess water.

2 Combine the oil, lemon juice and seasoning in a bowl. Add the bulgur wheat, then mix well, making sure all the grains are coated with the dressing. Let sit at room temperature for about 15 minutes so the bulgur wheat can absorb some of the flavors.

3 Stir in the chopped green onions, parsley, mint, tomatoes and feta. Taste and adjust the seasoning, adding more lemon juice to sharpen the flavor, if necessary.

4 Separate out the leaves from the radicchio and select the best cup-shaped ones. Spoon a little of the tabbouleh into each one. Arrange on individual plates or on a serving platter and garnish with flat leaf parsley sprigs.

Bresaola, Onion and Arugula Salad

INGREDIENTS

Serves 4
2 onions
5–6 tablespoons olive oil
juice of 1 lemon
12 thin slices bresaola
2–3 ounces arugula
salt and freshly ground black pepper

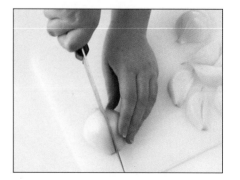

1 Slice each onion into eight wedges through the root.

2 Arrange the onion wedges in a single layer on a grill rack or in a flameproof dish. Brush them with a little of the olive oil and season well with salt and pepper.

3 Place the onion wedges under a hot broiler and broil them for 8–10 minutes, turning once, until they are just beginning to soften and turn golden brown at the edges.

4 Meanwhile, make the dressing: combine the lemon juice and 4 tablespoons of the olive oil in a small bowl. Add a little salt and black pepper and whisk well until the dressing is thoroughly blended.

5 If you have broiled the onions on a broiler rack, then transfer them to a shallow dish once they are done.

6 Pour about two-thirds of the dressing over the onion wedges and let cool.

7 When the onions are cold, arrange the bresaola slices on individual serving plates with the onions and arugula. Spoon on the remaining dressing and serve at once.

FRUIT SALADS

Fruit is always a fabulous way to end a meal.
In summer, a bowl of berries, such as Berry Salad, with
strawberries, raspberries, and blackberries, is as near perfection as
you are likely to get. In the fall and winter, when berries are
unavailable or just too expensive, try making compotes, such as
Autumn Fruit Salad, with its delicious blend of fruit and fruit juice.
Classic fruit salads, like Orange Salad, are perennial favorites, but
for something more exotic, try Persian Melon Salad, which has an
intriguing and delicate flavor.

Tropical Fruit Salad

INGREDIENTS

Serves 4–6
1 pineapple
1 can (14 ounces) guava halves
 in syrup
2 bananas, sliced
1 large mango, peeled, pitted and
 diced
4 ounces preserved ginger and
 2 tablespoons of the syrup
½ teaspoon ground cinnamon
½ teaspoon freshly grated nutmeg
coconut strips, to decorate

1 Peel, core and cube the pineapple, and place in a serving bowl. Drain the guavas, reserve the syrup and chop. Add the guavas to the bowl with one of the bananas and the mango.

2 Chop the ginger and add it to the pineapple mixture in the bowl.

3 Pour 2 tablespoons of the ginger syrup, and the reserved guava syrup into a blender or food processor and add the other banana, the coconut milk and the sugar. Blend to make a smooth creamy purée.

4 Pour the banana and coconut mixture over the fruit in the serving bowl. Add a little grated nutmeg and a sprinkling of cinnamon. Serve the fruit salad chilled, decorated with coconut.

Avocado Salad in Ginger and Orange Sauce

This is an unusual fruit salad since avocado is more often treated as a vegetable. However, in the Caribbean it is used as a fruit, which of course it is!

INGREDIENTS

Serves 4
2 firm ripe avocados
3 firm ripe bananas, chopped
12 fresh cherries or strawberries
juice of 1 large orange
shredded fresh root ginger (optional)

For the ginger syrup
2 ounces fresh ginger, chopped
3¾ cups water
1 cup light brown sugar
2 cloves

1 First make the ginger syrup: place the ginger, water, sugar and cloves in a saucepan and bring to a boil. Reduce the heat and simmer for about 1 hour, until well reduced and syrupy.

2 Remove the ginger and discard. Let cool. Store in a covered, clean container in the fridge.

3 Peel the avocados, cut into cubes and place in a bowl with the bananas and cherries.

5 Add a little shredded ginger, if using, then serve.

4 Pour the orange juice over the fruits. Add 4 tablespoons of the ginger syrup and mix gently, using a metal spoon. Chill the salad in the fridge for about 30 minutes.

Berry Salad

There are many things going for this stunning fruit salad: it can be made in advance; you can make larger quantities of it for parties; it looks superb and it tastes delicious.

INGREDIENTS

Serves 8

1 cup raspberries or
   blackberries
¼ cup red currants or
   black currants (optional)
2–4 tablespoons sugar
8 ripe plums
8 ripe apricots
1 cup seedless grapes
½ cup strawberries

1 Mix the berries and currants (except for the strawberries) with 2 tablespoons sugar. Pit the plums and apricots, cut them into pieces and put half of them into a pan with the berries.

2 Cook over very low heat with about 3 tablespoons water, or in a bowl with no water in the microwave, until the fruit is just beginning to soften and the juices are starting to run.

3 Let cool slightly and then add the reserved plums and apricots, and the grapes. Taste for sweetness and add more sugar if the fruit is too tart. Let the fruit salad cool, cover and chill – overnight if necessary.

4 Just before serving, transfer the fruit to a serving bowl. Slice the strawberries and arrange them over the fruit in the bowl.

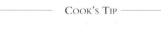

COOK'S TIP

Serve this delicious fruit salad with plain yogurt, fresh cream, crème fraîche or vanilla ice cream.

Melon and Grapefruit Salad

With its clean, refreshing taste and subtle sweetness, this is the perfect fruit salad. It is simple to make but elegant enough to grace any dinner party.

INGREDIENTS

Serves 4

1 small galia or ogen melon
1 small charentais melon
2 pink grapefruit
3 tablespoons orange juice
4 tablespoons sweet vermouth
seeds from ½ pomegranate
mint sprigs, to decorate

COOK'S TIP

Ugli fruit makes a good substitute for grapefruit. It is a hybrid of the orange, tangerine and grapefruit, with a yellowy-green skin. The skin is looser and easier to peel than that of a grapefruit and the flesh is deliciously sweet and juicy.

1 Halve the melons lengthwise and scoop out all the seeds. Cut into wedges and remove the skins, then cut across into large bite-size pieces.

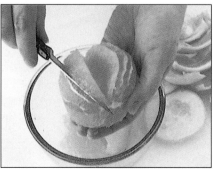

2 Using a small sharp knife, cut the peel and pith from the grapefruit. Holding the fruit over a bowl to catch the juice, cut between the grapefruit membranes to release the segments. Set aside the grapefruit segments.

3 Stir the orange juice and vermouth into the bowl containing the reserved grapefruit juice.

4 Arrange the melon pieces and grapefruit segments haphazardly on four individual serving plates. Spoon the mixed juices over the fruit, then scatter with the pomegranate seeds. Decorate with mint sprigs and serve immediately.

Persian Melon Salad

This is a typical Persian dessert, using a mixture of sweet fresh fruits flavored with rosewater and aromatic mint.

INGREDIENTS

Serves 4

2 small melons
1 cup strawberries, sliced
3 peaches, peeled and cut into small
  cubes
1 bunch seedless grapes (green or red)
2 tablespoons superfine sugar
1 tablespoon rosewater
1 tablespoon lemon juice
crushed ice
4 sprigs of mint and 4 strawberries, to
  garnish

1 Carefully cut the melons in half and remove the seeds. Scoop out the flesh with a melon baller, making sure not to damage the skin. Reserve the melon shells. Alternatively, if you don't have a melon baller, scoop out the flesh using a large spoon and cut into bite-size pieces.

2 Reserve four strawberries and slice the others. Place in a bowl with the melon balls, the peaches, grapes, sugar, rosewater and lemon juice.

3 Return fruit into the melon shells and chill in the fridge for 2 hours.

4 To serve, sprinkle with crushed ice, decorating each melon with a whole strawberry and a sprig of mint.

COOK'S TIP

To peel fresh peaches, cover them with boiling water and let stand for a couple of minutes. Rinse them under cold water before peeling.

Orange Salad

This classic fruit salad is a deserving favorite. It is light and simple-to-make, refreshing and delicious.

INGREDIENTS

Serves 4

4 oranges
2½ cups water
1½ cups sugar
2 tablespoons lemon juice
2 tablespoons orange blossom water
 or rosewater
½ cup pistachios, shelled and chopped,
 to garnish

1 Peel the oranges with a potato peeler down to the pith.

2 Cut the orange peel into fine strips and boil in water for several minutes to remove the bitterness. Drain and set aside until required.

3 Place the water, sugar and lemon juice in a saucepan. Bring to a boil, then add the orange peel and simmer until the syrup thickens. Add the orange blossom or rosewater, stir and let cool.

4 Completely peel the pith from the oranges and cut them into thick slices. Arrange in a shallow serving dish and pour the syrup over the fruit. Chill for 1–2 hours, decorate with pistachios and serve.

Emerald Fruit Salad

A contrasting mixture of fruits combine to make this a fruit salad with a difference.

INGREDIENTS

Serves 4
2 tablespoons lime juice
2 tablespoons honey
2 Granny Smith apples, cored and sliced
1 small honeydew melon, diced
2 kiwi fruit, sliced
1 star fruit, sliced
mint sprigs, to decorate
yogurt or whipped cream, to serve

1 Combine the lime juice and honey in a large bowl, then toss the apple slices in the mixture.

2 Stir in the melon, kiwi fruit and star fruit. Place in a glass serving dish and chill before serving.

3 Decorate the fruit salad with mint sprigs and serve with yogurt or whipped cream.

--- VARIATION ---

Add other fresh green fruits to this salad when available, such as plums, grapes, pears, or another kind of melon.

Autumn Fruit Salad

Despite the name, you can make a version of this fruit salad all year round – just change the fruit to suit the season.

INGREDIENTS

Serves 4

2 tablespoons sugar, plus extra
  to taste
juice of 1 lemon
1 Jonathan apple, cored and sliced
1 Granny Smith apple, cored
  and sliced
1 pear, peeled, cored and sliced
³/₄ cup apple or pear
  juice
4 plums, pitted and halved
  or quartered
4 ounces fresh raspberries, blackberries,
  blueberries or strawberries

1 Dissolve the sugar in the lemon juice in a large bowl. As you prepare the apples and pear, put them straight into the lemony syrup.

2 Pour the apple juice on top, cover the bowl tightly and leave in a cool place for 2–6 hours.

3 Shortly before serving, stir in the rest of the fruit and some more sugar to taste.

Melon and Strawberry Salad

This beautiful and colorful fruit salad is suitable to serve as a refreshing appetizer or to round out a meal.

INGREDIENTS

Serves 4

1 cantaloupe melon
1 honeydew melon
½ watermelon
1 cup fresh strawberries
1 tablespoon lemon juice
1 tablespoon honey
1 tablespoon chopped fresh mint
1 mint sprig (optional), to garnish

1 Prepare the melons by cutting them in half and discarding the seeds. Use a melon baller to scoop out the flesh into balls or a knife to cut it into cubes. Place the melon balls in a fruit bowl.

2 Rinse and take the stems off the strawberries, cut them in half and add them to the fruit bowl.

3 Combine the lemon juice and honey with about 1 tablespoon of water. Stir carefully to blend and then pour over the fruit. Stir the fruit so that it is thoroughly coated with the lemon and honey mixture.

4 Sprinkle the chopped mint over the top of the fruit. Serve garnished with the mint sprig, if desired.

COOK'S TIP

Use whatever melons are available: substitute galia for cantaloupe or charentais for watermelon, for example. However, try to find three different kinds of melon so that you get variation in color, and also a variety of textures and flavors.

Fruit Compote

Some of the best fruit salads are a mixture of fresh and dried fruits. This salad features some of the most delicious summer and winter fruits available, but you could experiment with almost any fruit – they combine together beautifully.

INGREDIENTS

Serves 4
4 ounces dried apricots
4 ounces dried peaches
4 ounces dried prunes
2 oranges, peeled and sliced

For the syrup
1 lemon
4 green cardamom pods
1 cinnamon stick
³/₄ cup honey
2 tablespoons ginger syrup from the jar
3 pieces preserved ginger

1 Soak the apricots, peaches and prunes in enough cold water to cover, for 1–2 hours, until they have plumped up.

2 Meanwhile, make the syrup. Pare two strips of rind from the lemon with a potato peeler or sharp knife. Halve the lemon and squeeze the juice from one half.

3 Lightly crush the cardamom pods with the back of a large, heavy-bladed knife.

4 Place the lemon rind, cardamom, cinnamon stick, honey, ginger syrup and lemon juice in a heavy saucepan. Add 4 tablespoons water, bring to a boil and simmer for 2 minutes. Set aside while making the fruit compote.

5 Drain the apricots, peaches and prunes and cut in half, or quarters if large. Place in a large pan with the oranges. Add 2 cups water, bring to a boil and simmer for 10 minutes until the fruit is tender.

6 Add the honey and ginger syrup, stir well and simmer for another 1–2 minutes. Allow the compote to cool, then chill it in the fridge for about 1–2 hours or overnight.

7 Chop the pieces of ginger and sprinkle them over the compote just before serving.

Mandarin and Orange Flower Salad

Mandarins, tangerines, clementines, mineolas: any of these lovely citrus fruits are suitable for this recipe.

INGREDIENTS

Serves 4
10 mandarins
1 tablespoon confectioners' sugar
2 teaspoons orange flower water
1 tablespoon chopped pistachios

1 Thinly pare a little of the rind from one mandarin and cut it into fine shreds for decoration. Squeeze the juice from two mandarins and reserve it.

2 Peel the remaining fruit, removing as much of the white pith as possible. Arrange the whole fruit in a wide dish.

3 Combine the reserved mandarin juice, sugar and orange flower water, then pour it over the fruit. Cover the dish and chill for at least 1 hour.

4 Blanch the shreds of mandarin rind in boiling water for 30 seconds. Drain, then let cool before sprinkling them over the mandarins, with the pistachios.

Minted Melon Salad

Here's a wonderful way to finish a meal. The melon is soaked in a luscious cocktail of fruit juices and liqueurs, but if you prefer you can make a non-alcoholic version by using extra fruit juice instead of tequila.

INGREDIENTS

Serves 4
2 melons, such as charentais,
   cantaloupe, galia or honeydew

For the cocktail syrup
³/₄ cup orange juice
³/₄ cup pineapple juice
½ cup tequila
1 tablespoon chopped fresh mint
1 tablespoon confectioners' sugar
mint sprigs, to decorate

VARIATION

Instead of tequila, use 4 tablespoons orange-flavored liqueur, such as Cointreau. Add 1 tablespoon honey to replace the confectioners' sugar.

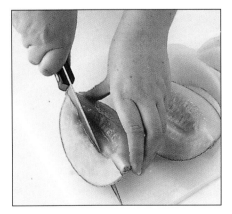

1 Halve the melons and scoop out the seeds using a metal spoon. Cut the melons into thin wedges using a sharp knife and remove the skins.

2 Arrange the two different varieties of melon wedges alternately on four individual serving plates.

3 Whisk the orange juice, pineapple juice, tequila, mint and sugar in a bowl, until the sugar has dissolved.

4 Pour the syrup over the melon and decorate with mint sprigs. Chill for about 30 minutes before serving.

Index